A NEW IRELAND

A NEW UNION.
A NEW SOCIETY.

A TEN YEAR PLAN?

Paul Gosling is a financial journalist and economic
commentator based in Northern Ireland

A NEW UNION: A NEW SOCIETY

Social, political and economic proposals for a New Ireland
By *Paul Gosling*

With contributions from *Tom Healy* and *Pat McArt*

Self published in 2018 by:
Paul Gosling
www.paulgosling.net

1st Edition 2018

ISBN: 978-1-5272-3261-7

Interior and Cover Design
by Mary Campbell
Printed by W&G Baird

A NEW UNION: A NEW SOCIETY

CONTENTS

"Some of my unionist friends are saying for the first time to me, 'exactly how would I be worse-off in a united Ireland' [compared to post-Brexit Britain]? The answer is they wouldn't be worse-off. The unionist majority will not be around for very much longer... nationalism is now energised. Brexit is an existential threat to the UK."

MIKE NESBITT,
former leader of the Ulster Unionist Party [1]

"Too many unionists take the longevity of the Union for granted."

PETER ROBINSON,
former leader of the Democratic Unionist Party [2]

"I am a constitutional nationalist, I would like to see a united Ireland in my lifetime. If possible, in my political lifetime."

SIMON COVENEY
Tanaiste [3]

1
INTRODUCTION

Northern Ireland is at a crucial point in its history. Since its creation in 1921, it has been led and dominated by unionism. But the situation has changed, significantly.

The Northern Ireland Assembly no longer has a unionist majority. Instead there is no clear majority for either tradition, with a casting vote held by assembly members that are cross-community. Except, the Assembly no longer functions. Members of the two main parties – the DUP and Sinn Fein – have little respect for each other. The Executive has not met since January 2017 and at the time of writing, there seems no prospect of them doing so.

A series of difficult political challenges apparently cannot be resolved through agreement by the two parties – these include an Irish language act, the misuse of the renewable heat incentive, gay marriage and women's reproductive rights.

These policy challenges come at a time when the demography of Northern Ireland is reflecting a major change. Within a few years, citizens from a Catholic background will outnumber those from a Protestant background. The parties that are nationalist and republican are, on balance, more socially liberal than those from a unionist affiliation. And younger voters seem more socially liberal and open minded than are older voters.

For all these reasons, Peter Robinson has called for unionists to recognise the threat to the union – that calls for a united Ireland will become more vocal and that a 'border poll' appears to be inevitable within a few years. If unionists want to preserve the union, they cannot rely either on history or 'identity politics'. They must provide evidence that justifies Northern Ireland's place within the union.

An increasing number of people from a unionist/Protestant background are sympathetic to the idea of Northern Ireland joining with the Republic to create a 'new Ireland'. For these, the economic growth of the southern Irish economy, the modernisation of the Irish state, its adoption of socially liberal policies on matters such as divorce, gay marriage and abortion and the marginalised role of the Catholic church in the operation of the state make it an increasingly attractive nation.

But this group of former unionists are very much still a minority within their community. For many Protestants/unionists/loyalists (PUL), it is identity and association with the United Kingdom that is more important than the social liberalism and economic strength of the south. What then, if anything, would encourage more members of the PUL community to accept and commit to a united, new, Ireland?

It is not just a question of union with GB versus a united Ireland, but a question of shaping a new society. On the one hand, only an Ireland that continues its modernisation will be attractive to even more people from Northern Ireland. On the other, Great Britain would need to strengthen its relationship with a united Ireland, in which Irish citizens' right to identify as British is recognised by both states. There needs to be close co-operation between the two neighbouring nations that reflects the truth that a mutually respectful partnership is the best, and most beneficial, way forward.

Changes that the Republic of Ireland would need to make for people with a British identity to feel more comfortable would include a health service free at the point of use, which is based on the UK's National Health Service, while operating more efficiently and effectively that does the NHS at present in Northern Ireland. There would need to be some constitutional reforms, to make clear the valued role of unionists within the new society. This might mean an Irish Bill of Rights, which incorporated protections enshrined in the Belfast Agreement/Good Friday Agreement.

This report makes clear, that change could happen through a border poll in which a majority of 50% plus one gets its way over a minority of 50% minus one. But that is a settlement that will be uncomfortable. And there is the risk of a majority in the north, but no majority for change in the south. Lessons must be learnt, as Peter Robinson has stressed, from the Brexit referendum. The vote for or against a united Ireland, when it comes, must be based on a realistic, fact-based, discussion of what would happen and what it means.

The aim of this report is to assist with the beginning of that conversation.

THANKS AND ACKNOWLEDGEMENTS

Sincere thanks are given to research co-ordinator Colm McKenna and colleague Pat McArt, without whom the project would not have been possible.

Further thanks are given to Tom Healy and Pat McArt for their contributions, to Mr Justice Richard Humphreys for giving permission to reproduce articles by him in the appendix and to Colm McKenna for his summary of the SláinteCare proposals.

The economic section of the report was heavily consulted upon and thanks are given to those who assisted. Responses (critical as well as positive) were received from Esmond Birnie, Ulster University; John Campbell, economics editor, BBC, Northern Ireland; Neil Gibson, senior economist, EY Ireland; and Richard Ramsey, chief economist for Northern Ireland, Ulster Bank. Thanks are also given to Des Murphy SC for his comments on constitutional matters.

Representatives of most of the political parties operating in Northern Ireland provided responses to the report, some on a not for publication basis, as did the Orange Order and the Irish Congress of Trade Unions. All these submissions have been carefully considered and earlier draft reports have been significantly amended in the light of these comments.

More than a hundred other responses were received by email, Twitter and in the opinion pages of Northern Ireland newspapers. A few were hostile or negative, but the vast majority of responses welcomed the beginning of a conversation that has become inevitable. Brexit, as well as changing demography, appears to have made the timing of that conversation imminent.

STRENGTHS AND WEAKNESSES OF THE TWO JURISDICTIONS

NORTHERN IRELAND

STRENGTHS
- Higher education sector
- NHS (in principle)
- Good quality of life
- Low cost of living

WEAKNESSES
- Lack of devolved government
- Administrative uncertainty
- Service duplication/sectarianisation
- Weak economy
- Brexit impact
- Public sector dependency
- High level of economic inactivity
- Too few graduates/undergraduates
- Inadequate vocational skills
- Too many without basic skills
- NHS (in practice)
- Lack of effective sub-regional policy
- Low productivity
- Poor infrastructure
- Substantial fiscal deficit
- Declining manufacturing sector
- Low wages
- Economic inequality

STRENGTHS AND WEAKNESSES OF THE TWO JURISDICTIONS

REPUBLIC OF IRELAND

STRENGTHS

- Stable government
- Strong economy
- Higher education sector
- Graduate skills
- High productivity
- Good infrastructure
- Falling fiscal deficit (near balanced budget)
- High, and growing, pay
- Open economy
- EU membership/EU funding
- High levels of FDI
- IFSC
- IDA

WEAKNESSES

- Still recovering from bank bail-out
- Brexit impact
- Poor/expensive health service
- Too many without basic skills
- Too few homes
- Inadequate sub-regional policy
- High cost of living
- Vulnerability to global trading conditions/eurozone
- Threats to tax rate from EU & US
- Economic inequality

2

THE TEN YEAR, TEN POINT PLAN

1

Negotiations should begin to agree objectively the actual size of the UK's subvention to Northern Ireland in advance of any poll to initiate a united Ireland. The UK government would be asked to agree to continue its subvention to Northern Ireland for a temporary period, phasing this out on an annually tapering basis, with the UK subvention removed entirely within a negotiated period beyond reunification. UK support might be needed for up to ten years, but with additional continuing support to meet the costs of pension liabilities for retired UK civil servants and other UK public sector workers, under an arrangement similar to that with EU withdrawal. Over the long term this would produce a significant fiscal gain for the UK, which is likely to be welcomed by taxpayers in GB. For Northern Ireland, the subsidy would be replaced by higher tax revenues as Northern Ireland benefits from the economic impact of reunification and the Republic's economic policies.

(Consideration could be given as to whether sovereignty might also transfer on a gradual basis. Stormont might continue to operate as a devolved assembly, but of Ireland rather than of the UK. There could be a phased move towards a truly all-island economy, with both sterling and the euro accepted by businesses during the transition process. Substantial efforts must be made to accommodate the fears and concerns of those who have a British or Ulster Scots identity throughout the island of Ireland in order that a successful unified economy is achieved.)

2 Increased spending on capital projects in Northern Ireland is required to bring infrastructure up to modern European standards. The infrastructure deficit that was carried forward from the period of direct rule needs to be addressed, which means that the UK government has an obligation to help meet the cost of correcting the infrastructure deficit. A UK government investment of £10bn would assist significantly with this, towards the cost of roads, health reform, education facilities and water and sewerage systems. This would recognise the absence of a 'peace dividend' following the Good Friday Agreement, which had been assumed. The possibility of a bridge connection with Scotland might be considered as a means to provide reassurance to unionists that economic, social and political connections with Great Britain could actually be strengthened through new arrangements.

3 A reduction in the number of civil servants in Northern Ireland to the same level as the Republic would assist in making Northern Ireland financially self-sufficient. This would take place on a gradual basis to reduce the impact on individuals and on the wider economy. Ideally the impact would be spread over several years, achieved as much as possible by natural wastage. All redundancy, pension and restructuring costs would be met by UK. This restructuring would assist in boosting Northern Ireland productivity. This transition would be part of the phased withdrawal of UK support for Northern Ireland.

4 The European Union would be asked to assist with the reunification of Ireland. A special case should be presented to the European Union for assistance with the cost and social pressures involved with Irish reunification. This might be structured in ways that learn from the Marshall Plan and the experience of German reunification. A new 32 county administration should use low cost loans from the European Investment Bank to invest in the economy and all-island infrastructure.

5 A political agreement on a new all island jurisdiction, inside the EU, would attract increased EU funding through Interreg, including financial assistance in restructuring Northern Ireland's infrastructure to improve its competitive position and integrated all-island economy.

6 IDA Ireland would promote all of the island on the world stage. This would produce benefits for all. Given its track record in attracting FDI worldwide it should prove to be a major player in turning the Northern Ireland economy into a world class competitor. Invest NI would be subsumed into IDA Ireland.

7 Improved direct links between education and industry in Northern Ireland as is the case in the Republic would lead to a more competitive market-oriented economy and increase employment rates.

8 While Northern Ireland needs to learn from the Republic with regards to elements of its education and skills system, the Republic needs to learn from Northern Ireland in terms of the cost and efficiency of its health system. Neither system is adequate at present. The Bengoa reforms[4] need to be implemented in Northern Ireland. An integrated all island health system, free at the point of delivery, is an essential prerequisite to achieving political integration.

9 A harmonised corporation tax rate would make all the island more attractive to foreign direct investment. This would also expand supply chains within, and across, the island, strengthening the internal economy in both the north and the south.

10 A single and integrated Ireland would create economies of scale and a more competitive economy. A single Ireland would be a world leader in the fields of research and development, higher education, pharmaceuticals and new technologies.

3
MOVING FORWARD

Whether in the foreseeable future Northern Ireland decides to become part of a united Ireland, or whether it continues as part of the UK, there must be a similar path to progress. A Northern Ireland that is a devolved part of the UK must achieve proper, generous reconciliation between different identities. This is equally true – arguably even more so – should Northern Ireland become part of a reunified Ireland.

The Good Friday Agreement was intended as the basis for creating a shared society, in which communities became integrated and reconciled. They would move on from the past. There was an expectation that there would be a peace dividend, which would create jobs and higher incomes. The failure of that ambition is illustrated by the gap between the employment rate (the percentage of working age adults in employment) in Northern Ireland and the rest of the UK, which has actually increased since the Good Friday Agreement. In some respects, Northern Ireland has fallen further behind Great Britain economically in the past 20 years, when the expectation was that the gap would close.

Peter Sheridan of Co-operation Ireland made the interesting proposal that a Department for Reconciliation should have been established by the Executive. Certainly the focus on reconciliation by the Executive was inadequate and arguably abandoned, with a willingness instead to accept what might be regarded as 'separate development'.

In 2010, the Joseph Rowntree Foundation published "*From a 'shared future' to 'cohesion, sharing and integration'*". This pointed out the damage caused by replacing the objective of 'reconciliation' with the lesser one of 'cohesion'. Mutual accommodation had become the aim, rather than tackling the roots and continuation of sectarianism. As one of our interviewees, lawyer Philip Gilliland, observed, voluntary segregation is not good enough. As a society, we need to heal. And that healing must encompass the whole of the island.

There is an interesting parallel here. Former deputy first minister Mark Durkan told us that one of the most regrettable reverses in the devolution process in Northern Ireland was the ending of the Civic Forum. It had been seen – particularly by the Women's Coalition – that the strengthening of civic society was an important step towards binding Northern Ireland together, while also creating a broader and more effective system of political accountability, which went beyond party politics.

In the Republic, the role of the Citizens' Assembly was hugely influential in putting forward an amendment to the constitution regarding abortion. A broader civic engagement has proved to be a progressive move in the Republic, and it is to be hugely regretted that Northern Ireland has moved away from this approach.

Alliance MLA and deputy leader Stephen Farry made an important observation in his interview with us, pointing out that it was the slow progress towards full implementation of the Good Friday Agreement that led to increased electoral support for the more hard line political parties. History cannot be reversed, but the current enforced period of reflection is a good moment to consider whether some elements of the Good Friday Agreement that have been abandoned should be re-evaluated, such as the Civic Forum (or a possible replacement citizens' assembly).

It is to be hugely welcomed that the DUP is itself going through a period of reflection. We have included points made by former DUP finance minister Mervyn Storey, who expressed a willingness for greater compromise in future government. He was not the only senior DUP member that we spoke with and it is clear that the DUP is very aware that it must be more inclusive in government if the Executive is to resume and work in the future. One of the points made by Mervyn Storey – and from others outside the DUP – was that he was unsure who really made decisions in Sinn Fein and this undermined trust within the Executive.

Part of the purpose of this report was to ask key influencers from different backgrounds what their core values were. The hope is that if we can focus on values, rather the community identities, it might be possible to make progress. It was heartening to have engagement from across the political spectrum.

A number of values were expressed repeatedly: 'reconciliation', 'respect', 'honesty', 'truth', 'rule of law', 'inclusion', 'equality' and 'justice'. Significantly, almost everyone said it was essential that government must be 'future focused' and concentrate on delivering agreed outcomes. It might be hoped that establishing a government around those values might assist with progress and stability.

There were some points of disagreement. Some said that 'trust' was essential, whereas Máirtín Ó Muilleoir suggested that it was possible to have government without mutual trust, providing there was agreement. However, this is presumably the reason why Stephen Farry referred to the Executive as having become a "transactional clearing house", with the key decisions taken outside of the room and just being rubber stamped in the Executive. It is important to stress, though, that Claire Sugden reported that this was not her experience when she was on the Executive in a later period. While Stephen Farry felt the minority parties were not treated with respect on the Executive, Claire Sugden felt that as the sole MLA from outside the two main parties she was well treated and regarded.

A view was also expressed that there were times when the two main parties got on better in private than they did in public. This, it would seem, may have been counter-productive. Both the main parties have had difficulty in bringing their party supporters with them at difficult times. Our society can only make progress if there is genuine reconciliation. For that to happen, there has to be the "brave leadership" that Claire Sugden called for. It requires the parties to be clear that they are against sectarianism and support social integration, including in schools and housing. We seem to be a long way from achieving that. It also requires the main parties to be unapologetic to their supporters about their commitment to work in partnership and to heal divisions.

Isolation within separate communities is not assisting reconciliation: it is also financially unsustainable. How long will the UK government – and taxpayers (particularly in England) - be willing to finance a large subvention to Northern Ireland? Much of that subvention meets the cost of the social division and service duplication that continues to mark Northern Ireland.

Ironically, while the choice between UK or UI represents the division between the DUP (and TUV and UUP) with Sinn Fein (and the SDLP), the symptoms of that division must be addressed irrespective of whether the north becomes part of an all-island Ireland, or continues to be Northern Ireland. For unionists, the costs of division must be addressed if the UK is to continue to be willing to pick up the bill. For republicans, they must demonstrate their capacity to be effective (and more effective than in the past) in government if they are to be in government in the south and to influence the debate around the reunification of Ireland.

One point made by several interviewees is that Sinn Fein cannot be the successful advocates of a united Ireland. History prevents them winning over many of the people that need to be won over. As former First Minister Peter Robinson hinted in a recent Queen's University lecture, the future requires a more reasoned debate over the future of Ireland than was achieved over Brexit. A compromise that keeps everyone happy with relation to the future of Northern Ireland is impossible. But to achieve the 'settled' outcome that will lead to an effective all-island state must require a significant number of Protestants, former unionists, to believe it is the best solution. Those people need to be won over by evidence.

A NEW IRELAND?

There was widespread agreement amongst those we interviewed that it would be unacceptable to expect Northern Ireland to join the Republic of Ireland as it stands. While its new social liberalism is widely welcomed across the north, its heavily criticised health system is unpopular in Northern Ireland. The housing crisis in the south is another negative. And while regional policy in the Republic is arguably better than that in the north, it is not effective enough.

"I think it is particularly valuable that the report points out that future arrangements in any new all island Irish State should draw from best practice in either jurisdiction, such as health in the North and economics and education in the Republic," commented Ray Bassett (former Irish Ambassador to Canada). "The NHS is needed in a united Ireland," said Claire Sugden. "We must have an NHS, free at the point of delivery," echoed Stephen Farry.

Academic Andy Pollak suggested: "The idea of an all-island health service is worth considering seriously. I believe this would be a practical and mutually beneficial 'pilot' project to see how wider all-island governance could work in the longer term."

As leading political commentator Brian Feeney put it: "If you just called a referendum it would be lost because no one knows at present what they're voting for: a unitary state, a federal state, a confederal state, the continuation of Stormont subordinate to the Dáil? What would the currency be? What would happen to health care? Would I have to pay €100 to go to A & E? What would the question(s) be in the referendum?"

THE ROLE OF THE IRISH GOVERNMENT

It is essential that there is a good relationship between the Irish state and the people and institutions of Northern Ireland. That applies irrespective of the constitutional situation of Northern Ireland. Brexit has created unhelpful, negatives stresses to those relationships. Taoiseach Leo Varadkar is making efforts to improve relationships with civic society in the north. But as Jane Morrice observed: "We need to improve the outreach from the south to unionists and Protestants in the north. This needs to be taken seriously – very seriously. Tokenism is not enough." The election of former Ulster Farmers' Union President Ian Marshall to the Senate is excellent and indicative of much more that needs to be done.

It would be helpful if many more people – the unionist population – looked to the Taoiseach as an advocate for their interests. As Máirtín Ó Muilleoir expressed it, "We need more 'Irish unionists' - unionists who see themselves as Irish." In truth, many unionists – as Claire Sugden elegantly explained – are comfortable as being both unionist and Irish, including by supporting the Irish rugby and cricket teams.

But for this progress to happen, change is needed in the south, to embrace not merely all the people of the north, but also to acknowledge the history of people of the north and the positive role of Protestants. "The rest of Ireland does not understand about the role of Presbyterianism, for example its role in creating the United States," explained Philip Gilliland, who is an historian as well as a lawyer. "This needs to be an all-Ireland conversation. Catholic Ireland needs to be proud of the Ulster Scots' contribution and welcome them into the family. That would be an historic meeting of minds. How do we get more people in Ireland educated about the Presbyterian role? Paisley was correct: two tribes have to get on. This is a ten year conversation. Protestant Ulster needs to go to Dublin to talk."

This progress must go beyond government. It should be noted, though, the warm praise from Bishop Ken Good for the generosity from the Department of Foreign Affairs in supporting the Church of Ireland. Jane Morrice made the profound observation that other Irish institutions must begin to see themselves as relevant to the whole of Ireland, including the north, if the people of Northern Ireland are to see the Republic as relevant to them. "The institutions in the Republic need to reflect more of the northern culture, for example, RTE," she argued, persuasively. "RTE does not have much presence in the north and its broadcasts are not easily accessible in Northern Ireland. This restricts the level of knowledge and understanding in the north of the Republic's state and government."

Northern Ireland would be financially better-off as part of a reunified Ireland. But this is not a short-term project. While one recent opinion poll commissioned by the BBC showed significant support for a united Ireland, this is not a consistent result of all polls. And there remains much uncertainty around what people would be voting for. There needs to be an informed, open, debate on the merits of UK or UI. That debate should begin now. However, an immediate border poll might be to the benefit of those unionists who are strongly opposed to reunification and would like an early referendum that they are more likely to win and which might put the issue into a closed cupboard for several years.

It is instructive that most opinion leaders spoken with said that they did not have a clear picture of what a united Ireland would look like. Mark Durkan had both a vision and a route map towards achieving it. His plan includes clarity that Northern Ireland would become part of the existing Republic of Ireland, as a new constitution created too much uncertainty - voters within the Republic might find that much change unacceptable. He also believes that there must be bold measures to protect British identities. These include the right to continue to hold a British nationality and identity after reunification.

Part of the useful ongoing debate would focus on whether the Republic should become federated, with the continuation of Stormont – and whether Stormont should be for the existing six counties, or the nine counties of Ulster. If the latter, should there also be assemblies for the other provinces? Would Stormont, and other possible assemblies, have the existing or lesser powers?

There are also issues around community identities that this section of the report has attempted to steer away from. These include flags, emblems, parades, relationships with the British Crown, the role of the President, languages. If these could be discussed as part of an early theoretical debate, rather than later on as part of a real decision-making process, the level of contention and tension might be reduced.

Perhaps the first priority, though, if the Republic is genuinely committed to eventual reunification is the reform of its health service. The cost of reform would be substantial in moving to a free at point of delivery model, but discussions around this change have now begun and could usefully progress as a matter of urgency. Failure to do so would be regarded by many in the north as an impediment to reunification.

As the main parties ally themselves closely with Christian values, it might be appropriate to quote Bishop Ken Good's comments. "Generosity needs to be shown. As Christians, we need to be proactive with forgiveness. This has been overlooked. Christianity has forgiveness at its heart."

Perhaps the most telling remark made by an interviewee was from DUP MLA Mervyn Storey. Talking in general about Northern Irish society, he said: "There will be change." He then added: "I am against a single Irish jurisdiction – but I would have to accept it if there was a vote and that was the outcome. Unionists must not think that day could not come. There has to be an honest discussion around the benefits or disadvantages of being in the UK or a united Ireland. The reports, along with others, can inform a discussion. There is a lesson from what is happening in the Republic for everyone, including in unionism."

4
HOW IRELAND NEEDS TO CHANGE – VIEWPOINTS ON A NEW IRELAND

PETER SHERIDAN
Chief Executive, Co-operation Ireland

"The core values for transition out of violence are: peace keeping; peace making, peace building (which is where we are now) and peace sharing (which we have not yet reached).

"We have got through the peace making phase. We reached an agreement on how we are governed. But we have not agreed about how we learn to live together. We remain in a cold war situation. We had 18 peace walls before the Good Friday Agreement, we have 88 now. The institutions of the Good Friday Agreement were only ever supposed to be stepping stones to the next stage. Sectarianism is still there. Politicians are not genuinely committed to the Good Friday Agreement.

"People should ask the political parties what they are going to do. Ask unionists what they will do for nationalist and republicans. Ask republicans what will do to protect PUL communities. Good rights are what you will do to protect others. We have never got to the stage where we can walk in other people's shoes. But the good news is that everything is shift-able.

"We have to deal with the past. We need to debate the past and deal with it. Universities are a good place for debates. We will never do justice on the scale of the injustice. There should have been a Department for Reconciliation within the Executive. We should have had a future facing government. We don't do enough to tell unionists that we will protect unionist identity. We need to convince a generation of young people."

PHILIP GILLILAND
Lawyer and Anglican

"My values are those of the Taoiseach: socially liberal; fiscally, moderately conservative. I believe people should live according to the values they espouse, without hypocrisy and with tolerance. I believe in inclusion, including all indigenous and non-indigenous communities. In Northern Ireland, that explicitly means educating children together - otherwise people will never escape their 'mono-ness'.

"Sinn Fein does not articulate what it means by 'equality'. It can mean nothing more than our tribe must have the same as the other tribe. Equality can mean meritocracy, equality of opportunity - which is what we must strive towards. What does justice mean? We need truth and honesty about the past. Administratively, justice in respect of Troubles-related crimes is not possible. The forgotten people are the victims. What we need is truth. We need that from government and from republicans and from loyalists.

"We are in a system of voluntary segregation. Better government would help to deal with this and could lead to a process of desegregation. But who can govern us to lead us into desegregation? The only solution that we have not tried is for the Republic to do this.

"The UK government is not interested in direct rule and has no appetite for this. We need to explore another approach that could work and that is a united Ireland. Brexit has changed everything. It has helped Protestants to talk about a united Ireland in ways they never have before. Protestant business leaders are now talking about Brexit changing things. The east around Belfast is much more of a British economy, but the west is much less.

"As a Protestant it makes me wonder what it was about a united Ireland that we are supposed to be afraid of. For unionists a hundred years ago my guess is that their views were informed by three things:

1   Why leave the world's largest trading bloc,
2   Home rule would be Rome rule,
3   Bigotry.

"The theocracy is now in Northern Ireland, not the Republic of Ireland, which is a socially liberal country. Numbers one and two no longer apply, which only leaves number three and I don't want to be a bigot.

"The rest of Ireland does not understand about the culture and heritage of Ulster Scots Presbyterianism, for example its role in the creation of the United States. This needs to be an all-Ireland conversation. Catholic Ireland needs to be proud of the Ulster Scots' contribution and welcome them back into the family. That would be an historic meeting of minds. How do we get more people in Ireland educated about the Presbyterian role?

Paisley was correct on one thing: the two tribes have to find a way to get on. This is a ten year conversation. Protestant Ulster needs to go to Dublin to talk.

"I want a unitary Ireland, not a federal Ireland. A federal Ireland would do very little for the North West/Derry, which desperately needs to see the removal of the border. I would be against the continuation of Stormont for this reason, and also because the inherent tribal stalemate means it cannot function in anything other than a populist fashion. It would be different if it was a nine counties Stormont.

"How does it happen? If it's initiated by Catholic politicians, it can't happen. It has to come from Protestant NI and from Dublin."

MERVYN STOREY MLA
Former DUP Finance Minister

"I want a peaceful, settled, prosperous Northern Ireland. We are not living in the 1960s. There will be change. We need to be future focused. While I'd like past crimes to be dealt with through the courts, there is little chance sadly in many cases of getting justice for most past crimes. We've had a conflict management process, rather than a reconciliation process. There is the challenge.

"There was too much focus on the relationship between Ian Paisley and Martin McGuinness. We (in the DUP) don't know who is in charge of Sinn Fein. Too many unionists do not understand the dynamics and difficulties within republicanism. Too many unionist voters do not understand the differences between dissidents and Sinn Fein.

"The society I would like is: respect for the rule of law; fairness, for example in employment. There should be responsibility and accountability in government. I want devolution to work. A caring society that supports people in crisis.

To move beyond the platitudes of respect. I am anti-abortion and pro-traditional marriage, but I must recognise that others in my community have different views from me in this. Government in future should be outcomes focused.

"I am against a single Irish jurisdiction – but I would have to accept it if there was a vote and that was the outcome. Unionists must not think that day could not come. There has to be an honest discussion around the benefits or disadvantages of being in the UK or a united Ireland. The reports [in this series], along with others, can inform a discussion. There is a lesson from what is happening in the Republic for everyone, including in unionism."

CLAIRE SUGDEN MLA
Independent Unionist and former Justice Minister

"The values I want in society are respect, the appreciation that everyone is different and for that difference to be embraced. Difference can be contentious. I want empathy and compromise. You can't get agreement if you don't have empathy. It needs to be understood that we are the products of our experiences and of our families. I understand why people did things, even if I don't agree with what they did. I do have a specific designation as a unionist and I think that is right. We need to de-sensitise the concepts of unionism and nationalism.

"Justice is about upholding the rule of law. Often what people mean by justice is fairness. Truth is also difficult, because it means different things for different people. Social justice is another important concept. The different narratives should be told.

"My unionism is practical. I believe the best place for Northern Ireland for now is part of the UK. I am not convinced that even after Brexit that the best place for Northern Ireland will be outside the UK. If there were circumstances in which on a practical basis we would be better off in a united Ireland then I would consider that. Unionism is also part of my culture. Northern Ireland is my home and I wouldn't leave. I'm happy to say that I'm Irish, Northern Irish and British. The Good Friday Agreement allows us to say that we are both Irish and British. The Good Friday Agreement is not the end game for those pursuing nationalism. In 1998, Unionism thought that it was the compromise of both ideologies; nationalism saw it as a stepping stone. I am interested in the ideas of a 'new Ireland'; I'm not sure how those proposing it will find a purpose for unionism after unification.

"There was never contention on the [NI] Executive. The relationship was good between me, the DUP and Sinn Fein. Martin McGuinness nominated me as justice minister – he didn't need to do that, he could have just gone along with the nomination. I ensured that statements on justice involved the Executive as a whole, not just myself. The Executive was great. But now the party leaderships need to rein in their parties.

"Paramilitary violence now is more about community control and criminality, rather than politics. After the Good Friday Agreement we didn't effectively address problems, we just threw money at them. We need to be braver in dealing with the problems. Sinn Fein has secured the next generation of voters because of their social policies; the DUP needs to rethink their values in the context of a changing world and changing demographics in order to secure their vote and unionism's vote.

"The NHS is needed in a united Ireland. Sinn Fein needs to go on a journey. What I like about the Republic is that it is structured around issues, like the Department for Children. It is very focused on outcomes. And I like the voluntary coalition structure in the south. The Republic is being brave, for example on abortion and same sex marriage. It is helping Ireland move forward. I crave leadership in Northern Ireland."

RAY BASSETT
Former Irish Ambassador to Canada.

"The [earlier] report [in this series on the all-island economy] is very timely as the circumstances which led to the division of Ireland have radically changed, particularly in regard to economics and demographics. There has been a curious lack of debate on how the two parts of Ireland should react to the changed circumstances.

"I think it is particular valuable that the report points out that future arrangements in any new all island Irish State should draw from best practice in either jurisdiction, such as health in the North and economics and education in the Republic. I hope this report stimulates further serious study and discussion on a subject which was unfortunately taboo in the Republic for far too long."

IAIN BARR

Manager of Waterside Theatre, Derry/Londonderry,
community activist, son of senior loyalist Glen Barr

"I believe everyone should be treated equally and I am dismayed by what I see in Northern Ireland today. For example the abortion debate in the south has thrown up some strange bedfellows here, like the DUP and the Catholic Church. I find it amazing that a country such as the Republic of Ireland, which until very recently was basically governed by the Catholic Church, is now more liberal than Northern Ireland. We are now being shown as the 'backward' part of this island. These groups are opposed to equality: the DUP says it wants Northern Ireland to be the same as the rest of the UK but not when it comes to issues like same sex marriage or abortion.

"My father in the 70s wrote a document for a devolved system of government that got rid of green and orange politics and for sharing power. That remains the blueprint, the correct approach. A lot of politicians should mind their language. Politicians here are not leading. We can't move forward until we stop looking back."

BISHOP KEN GOOD

Church of Ireland, Bishop of Derry and Raphoe

"Ecclesiastically, the Church of Ireland is an all-Ireland entity: we pray for the Queen on one side of the border, for the President on the other. Some parishioners strongly identify with the UK, others with the Republic of Ireland. In church terms, the border is not paramount: as Christians, our prior loyalty must be to the Kingdom of God.

"The Department of Foreign Affairs funds some Church of Ireland activities in the north. There is a financial generosity in their approach. Some Republic of Ireland government ministers are very generous to the Church of Ireland. In the Republic, our Church is given more weight than our numbers may warrant. People [in RoI] are willing to listen to the Church of Ireland. Leo Varadkar and other ministers met with Protestant Church leaders recently and the Church of Ireland does feel valued. It is not necessarily a bad thing that the state has become more secular.

"My values include a concern that people of different religious and other traditions feel they have a place, that there is room for them, that they are valued, not exploited. Justice. Fairness. Inclusion. Respect.

"The treatment of victims is one of the biggest issues. Brave moves are needed on both sides. Generosity needs to be shown. As Christians, we need to be more proactive with forgiveness. This has been overlooked. Christianity has forgiveness at its heart."

GERALDINE CONAGHAN
Lawyer, Donegal

"I see merit in our recognising ourselves as part of the British Isles, but we [could] have a new confederation of the Island of Ireland and Scotland within the EU under a new constitution (scrap the 1937 version), and let England and Wales Brexit. The discussion has to be put out in the mainstream of ordinary citizens who care about the economy more and our future, but could NI with its top heavy civil service and politicians survive without UK funds? This is where Europe needs to step up and prop up the new Union within their larger Union."

JIM DORNAN
Professor

"Over the past months I have been very impressed how many people traditionally of a unionist background have come round to believe that a New Union of Ireland is the way forward. All who aren't historically and emotionally committed to a New Union truly need to see what's actually on offer before voting."

BRIAN FEENEY
Writer and Political Commentator

"This paper [the earlier report on the all island economy] on Irish unity emphasises engaging Unionists and offering them participation at all levels which must be the only way to proceed. However, the main immediate task is to engage the Irish government and its officials, many of whom are hostile to proposals for unity partly because they are incumbents and naturally resist change, partly because of laziness, partly because of fear of change, because of cost, but mostly for fear of the unknown.

"Finally, nothing can happen until Brexit is resolved. That means 2021 at the earliest. Governments can only manage one item as huge as Brexit at a time without contemplating major constitutional change as well. There will also be an Irish and a British general election, the first in 2019 or earlier, the second in 2022 at the latest. However, that means now is the right time to start planning for the future instead of being surprised by events."

BILLY PATTERSON
Southern Protestant and musician

"It is not possible that two groups of representatives who dislike one another intensely can be expected to go into business together even though it makes economic sense and both sides will benefit from the merger. They must become friends or at least respect one another before that can happen.

"I like the idea of letting the people on both sides know, if they don't already, of the number of Protestants from the Republic who were patriots, writers, musicians, poets, politicians, sportspeople, etc. and make them aware of little facts which might baffle the people of the Orange persuasion - the Pope sent King Billy a letter of congratulations after the Battle of the Boyne and a Mass of Deliverance was celebrated in Rome for his victory. History is often manipulated to suit the audience, so maybe it's time to tell the full story even though a lot of it is unpalatable.

"Ban religion from politics. Recognise each other's big marching days and support each other as they actually did in the 'old' days - pre 1916. AOH and Orange marches should not be permitted in areas where offence may be caused. Nationalists need to stop flying our tricolour in NI. A new flag is needed for all the people, which pleases the two main protagonists. Perhaps a green and orange flag with a harp on the green and a red hand on the orange. A new All-Ireland national anthem is recommended. New words even to the existing tune would be good. As it is, the words are archaic and hopefully there are alternatives to canon's roar and rifle's peal in the Ireland of tomorrow. I would see no future in recognising any language except the one spoken by everyone in the country - English. They must stop squabbling about trivia and get down to governing. References to past history should be avoided as they inhibit progress."

ANDY POLLAK
Founding director of the Centre for Cross Border Studies

"I like (former Attorney General) John Rogers' suggestion that the Irish Constitution should be amended to recognise 'the plural origins of our people'. People in the South are going to have to get used to the idea that in the event of unity constitution, flag and anthem (in order to incorporate 'Britishness' into Irish symbols) will all have to change. It won't be easy to persuade them.

"I also like (Senior Counsel) Des Murphy's idea of an independent international mediator (or maybe an international Opsahl-style commission) that could draw up proposals for the future governance of Ireland (within the framework of the Good Friday Agreement) - to be put to people north and south in a referendum. I would regard this as much more sensible than a crude Border Poll, which, in the event of a 50%+1 vote for unity, would lead to renewed mayhem.

"The idea of an all-island health service is also worth considering seriously. I believe this would be a practical and mutually beneficial 'pilot' project to see how wider all-island governance could work in the longer term.

"On the wider issue I think it needs to be spelled out just what an extraordinarily liberal society the Republic has become in a short time. It is now one of the most liberal countries in Europe: liberal abortion and same sex marriage overwhelmingly passed by referenda; gay, half-Indian Taoiseach; over 17% of the population foreign-born and not a whiff of a right-wing reaction."

JANE MORRICE

Former Women's Coalition MLA and deputy speaker of NI Assembly, former head of the European Commission's Office in Belfast, former NI deputy equality commissioner, Initiator of petition for NI to remain part of the EU.

"The values I want in society are honesty, integrity, equality, human rights, inclusion, mutual respect, understanding, tolerance, justice. Those values are European-wide and not linked to being north or south of the border.

"Reconciliation across the island is essential. I was present at the recent all-island forum on Brexit in Dundalk, which Barnier attended, but unionists were poorly represented. Outreach from the south to unionists and Protestants in the north should perhaps be more creative. This needs to be taken seriously – very seriously. Tokenism is not enough. Ian Marshall joining the Senate is good, but we have been here before with northern unionists sitting in the Senate.

"The institutions in the Republic need to reflect more of the northern culture, for example, RTE. RTE does not have much presence in the north and its broadcasts are not easily accessible in Northern Ireland. This restricts the level of knowledge and understanding in the north of the Republic's state and government."

JAMES WILSON

Historian and former British army soldier

"Since the Good Friday Agreement, the more regional identities such as Northern Irish have become more established - similar devolved regional identities have emerged in Wales and Scotland (the English are always English, even when they mean British). By 2010 the Life and Times survey was rating Northern Irish as high as a third of population. My kids and I have both passports and 'Norn Irish' is how we describe ourselves. My current research reveals a diversity of identity - even amongst passionate loyalists to the Crown.

"The Citizens' Assembly/Constitutional Convention convened [in Ireland] by Tom Arnold, has proved to be a very useful tool in unpacking sensitive subjects and framing debates such as the Eighth Amendment. Given the growing calls in the North for a border poll, would it not be prudent to task such a Citizens' Assembly to conduct a full open and lucid debate on the National Question, the reunification of Ireland, or indeed any other constitutional options – the best of British / the best of Irish - that can provide an agreed settlement?"

MARK DALY
Irish senator

"There is a need for action now, policy neglect seldom goes unpunished. The future is a united Ireland as provided for under the Good Friday Agreement, with protection for the culture and identity of unionists and within the European Union. The Good Friday Agreement is, in effect, the pathway to the peaceful and prosperous unity of Ireland and her people."

MÁIRTÍN Ó MUILLEOIR MLA
former Sinn Féin finance minister

"We need to adopt the values appropriate for a wounded society. The priorities should be: build the peace, foster reconciliation. There are lots of divided societies in Europe. But while there are divisions, those are different. No one has a clear answer on how to achieve this. Justice. You can't have reconciliation without justice. Which also means civil rights. You have to look forward, not live in the past. The Stormont House Agreement found a way to deal with justice, while moving forward. There's a balance.

"The aspirations for a united Ireland should be: prosperity; a shared future, which includes prosperity for all; no dysfunction, no peace walls, people should be safe to walk where they want; the normalising of peace; a modern European society. We should be international leaders. Ireland should be global in outlook.

"How to move ahead? We need more 'Irish unionists' - unionists who see themselves as Irish. No one has set out the form a united Ireland would take. I don't believe it would be like East Germany joining West Germany, it would be more complex.

"The future depends on the people who are proud of being Irish while being unionists, not those who despise the Irish language and are difficult to deal with. Irish unionism is a good tradition.

"My learnings as mayor of Belfast were that if you meet unionists half way, they will meet you; unionists are ahead of their political leadership; there is a real desire for change. I found people more welcoming than might be expected.

"It is possible to do deals without trust. There has to be a trade-off. Reaching out to unionism is an urgent task. We are not doing enough to build that bridge. There are big challenges for Sinn Féin.

"No one has really imagined the future. For example, how the Dáil would work, for example unionists in government. I would find it easier to imagine unionists in a continuing Stormont Assembly. The Good Friday Agreement was only a staging post. I have never thought about the role of the DUP and UUP in the Dáil. The collapse of the Executive is damaging for everyone, especially for the North West, for example regarding Magee. There is a real consequence, for example loss of funding for groups and services. Our vote may go up because of the collapse, but it is damaging to politics."

STEPHEN FARRY MLA
Deputy leader of the Alliance Party
Former employment minister

"I have a liberal perspective, which is a flexible term. I believe in rights, equality, fairness, a rights-based approach, empowerment, democracy, the rule of law. There is some disengagement from the rights agenda, for example equal marriage, LGBT rights, reproductive health care.

"Northern Ireland is still marked by sectarian division. This leads to different people having different life chances and can determine where they can live.

"The Good Friday Agreement was about creating new relationships across the islands, but it was imperfect. It was a means towards a reconciled and peaceful society. There were unresolved issues at the time - decommissioning was too slow, legacy, the rule of law - and these caused difficulties. That led to greater support for parties that took a hard line. There was no shared vision. Support for progress was always limited and qualified. In particular this was because the parties had different constitutional objectives.

"The Executive became a transactional clearing house. Lots of policy was determined outside the Executive. Proposals for health service reform were not discussed inside the Executive. Meetings were often unpleasant. There was little conversation about how do we deal with the big issues. The 'zero sum game' led to cronyism and lack of accountability, which in part contributed to the collapse.

"There was a conscious effort to keep constitutional issues out of the Executive, such as legacy, flags. These issues were discussed in other places. There was never a conversation at the Executive about segregation. It was about doing business as quickly as possible and get out. Meetings might be delayed by two, three or four hours and then the meeting last just ten minutes. One meeting that was scheduled for 2.30 actually began at 7.30. The Budget for 2016/17 for £11bn was tabled 30 minutes before the meeting and agreed on the nod.

"Sinn Fein were not very good at government. Lots of things had to be run through the wider party. This was difficult for them as a party of change. There was a lack of generosity by DUP to Sinn Fein and to other parties, especially after 2012. The draft agreement in February seems to show that Sinn Fein does want to be in government. But it does seem as if there is support for continuation of the Executive as a transactional clearing house. The DUP now looks more closely to London.

"On the question of reunification, I am open minded. I don't have a fixed mind regarding UK or united Ireland. We must have reconciliation, a liberal society. The Alliance contains some members who are unionists and others who are nationalist.

"Against: subvention is a powerful economic argument. We must have an NHS, free at the point of delivery. Pro: Brexit, especially a hard Brexit; a united Ireland provides a route back into the EU; social policy, RoI is rapidly changing and more attractive than NI. I am reconsidering my position. Any discussion risks polarising society. So we don't want to jump in. The present priority is delivery via a NI Executive. The tipping point would be a hard Brexit and bad economic outcomes would be influential. Northern Ireland is not yet ready for this discussion. Nothing is guaranteed on the future of the subvention, or whether there will be change to the Barnett Formula.

"I have not really thought about what the future would be in a united Ireland. There needs to be respect for British and Irish identities. Not simply assimilation. There needs to be change on both sides.

"If it happened, a lot of people in NI would be very unhappy. It might involve a constitutional settlement with unionist representatives and protection of the unionist population and their rights. There might be a consociational structure in UI, as in Belgium, where things are done in accordance with a convention. Northern Ireland does it constitutionally."

MARK DURKAN
former SDLP MP, leader and Finance Minister

"The Good Friday Agreement provides for two choices on the constitutional status of Northern Ireland - United Kingdom or a united Ireland. Unionist and nationalist aspirations are equally legitimate, therefore the threshold for majority consent in a referendum for either option must be equal. True parity of esteem cannot require a larger majority for one consent-based option rather than the other.

"Neither Unionists nor Nationalists would be working for just a 50% plus one outcome. Each would hope for bigger margins! But in the event of a narrow margin either way, the result has to be respected.

"The SDLP set out in papers (in 2003 and 2005) that the Good Friday Agreement must be seen to endure beyond any referendum result. In the event of a vote to change the north's constitutional status, the principles, promises and precepts of the Agreement should still hold as mandated in 1998. The Agreement provides for 'review' arrangements. Such review mechanisms would be the channels for adjustments to be made in institutional structures to be compatible with change in constitutional status and to remain compatible with the Agreement.

"We set this out to allay any apprehension that having a referendum or its possible outcome would forfeit the unique standing of the Agreement. We also did it to show that it was not just Unionists who were challenged by the Agreement to recondition their assumptions. This was a way of showing that Nationalists had to look at a united Ireland under the light of the Agreement. This means allowing for a continuing Strand One and embedding Strand Three's East-West structures for the future (using reviews to enhance these).

"There could not be a purely internal settlement in the north or inside the UK. But we can also accept that, even in a united Ireland, there would not be a purely internal settlement on this island. To take account of

Unionists' identity and ongoing affinity we have to think about more than just British passports for those who want them. As we have sought a direct northern voice in a reformed Seanad, then the "do unto others..." rule should apply in a united Ireland. This would not mean all institutions staying static in a united Ireland as a new dynamic would be created by the scale of northern representation in an all-Ireland parliament as compared with Westminster. That would include a substantive unionist presence.

"Recalibrating the devolution envelope and re-gearing for all-island administration and legislation can be achieved by agreement using the modalities of the Agreement, building confidence and furthering reconciliation on the island and between these islands.

"This sort of understanding avoids the false precondition of having to secure Unionist agreement to a united Ireland before a referendum. It also avoids the false promise of having a referendum which, if passed, only invites negotiations which could be frustrated. The Brexit negotiation debacle is a warning that those who value the unity by consent precept of the Agreement need to have a sat-nav for how a positive result is advanced consistent with the Agreement."

5

THE POLITICS OF IRELAND: PREPARING FOR REUNIFICATION

O nce it seemed as if the Republic of Ireland was to be governed in perpetuity by Fianna Fail governments, working in apparent partnership with the Catholic Church – interspersed by occasional periods in which Fine Gael attempted to lead minority governments. The global financial crash of 2008 destroyed the Celtic Tiger and the concepts both of Fianna Fail political dominance and the fiscal reputations of Charlie McCreevy, Bertie Ahern and Brian Cowen. Things had changed.

A Fine Gael government has ushered in a period of social liberalism marking a definitive separation of state and church. It has also indicated that the least republican of Ireland's major parties is now much more open – in the context of post-Brexit relationships – to Irish reunification.

"The EU needs to prepare for a united Ireland," explained then Taoiseach Enda Kenny, addressing the McGill Summer School in Glenties, Co. Donegal, in 2017. Leo Varadkar endorsed the comment, prior to himself leading the government, saying: "I share the vision of An Taoiseach that foresees a united Ireland at some point in the future, and I share his belief in how it should be achieved."[5] Tanaiste Simon Coveney has since gone further. "I am a constitutional nationalist, I would like to see a united Ireland in my lifetime. If possible, in my political lifetime."[6]

Senator Mark Daly of Fianna Fail argues that the outcome of a referendum must be understood before any poll takes place. "The lesson of Brexit is this: you do not have a referendum and then tell everybody what the future looks like," he said. "You only have a referendum at the end of a long, long process where you debate all the issues. We've got to prepare, and we've got to prepare now. Events take over, and politicians forget this."[7] In other comments, Daly said: 'it's a matter of record that the Dublin government has a policy to put to unionists in regard to unity. It's a clear case of failing to prepare is preparing to fail. Policy neglect rarely goes unpunished."

Peter Robinson is one Northern Ireland politician who has not ignored this. In an opinion article published in the Belfast Telegraph, he warned unionists not to take their affiliation to the United Kingdom for granted. "I do not believe calling a referendum would be justified and I have never called for it - indeed I have argued how distracting and destabilising it would be - but no amount of grandstanding changes the fact that unionists cannot stop it happening," he warned his supporters. "What I have sought is that unionists should be actively getting the rules and procedures concerning the conducting of a border poll and its aftermath sorted out to their satisfaction – now."[8]

Increasingly, politicians are also considering the possibility that demographic change, political evolution in the south and the likely impact of Brexit has meant that it has become conceivable that voters in Northern Ireland might within the foreseeable future support Irish reunification. Many in Britain would not object to this. Kevin Meagher is a former special advisor to Labour secretary of state for Northern Ireland, Shaun Woodward, and author of 'A United Ireland: why unification is inevitable and how it will come about'. He wrote: "Bluntly, Northern Ireland, with a population of just 1.8 million people, is of no strategic economic importance to Britain, representing just two per cent of the UK's GDP. Northern Ireland's best bet, economically, is to join with the South and align its economy to benefit from the Republic's strong record of attracting foreign direct investment."[9]

UK governments have been more equivocal, and inconsistent, about their strategic interest in terms of Northern Ireland. In 1990, the then secretary of state for Northern Ireland Peter Brooke said that "the British Government has no selfish strategic or economic interest in Northern Ireland". This position was reaffirmed by John Major as prime minister in 1993 in the Downing Street Declaration, when he again made clear "on the behalf of the British Government, that they have no selfish strategic or economic interest in Northern Ireland."[10] The statement was supported by the then leader of the opposition, Tony Blair, who carried the policy into government, which was implemented as part of the understanding behind the Belfast Agreement (Good Friday Agreement).

Since then, Theresa May has seemed to shift government policy away from neutrality in the event of a reunification referendum. May is dependent on the DUP for a majority in the House of Commons, which may explain her, in effect, changing the policy of government. In the event of a border poll, said May, a government led by her would argue for Northern Ireland remaining part of the UK. "I believe in the partnership of our four great nations in one proud Union and I want it to endure for generations to come. So a government I lead will never be neutral in our support for the Union. We will always make the case for it."[11]

Despite this, many people believe that the mood is shifting amongst what might be regarded as 'soft unionism'. Tony Blair's trusted advisor Jonathan Powell commented: "You do hear stories of middle-class unionists in the golf and the rugby clubs saying 'if we're going to leave the EU, we might as well stay in as a United Ireland'. Friends of mine tell me they're hearing this. You'd have never have heard that before."[12]

Ever since the foundation of the Irish state, consideration has been given to reunification. And it was also recognised that an eventual settlement may need to involve some type of devolution or federation. In 1921 Eamon de Valera declared: "We are ready to give such local autonomy to Ulster...as would be practicable, if it would make for the contentment and satisfaction of the residents there."

But there has also been a recognition that change could only happen gradually and when the circumstances meant that it made sense.

Rostrevor-born T.K. Whitaker was the top civil servant in the Republic when the Troubles broke out in 1968. He advised then Taoiseach, Jack Lynch, to adopt a policy of "patience, understanding and forbearance" when dealing with unionism. Whitaker told Lynch: "The most forceful argument in favour of the patient good neighbour policy aimed at ultimate 'agreement in Ireland between Irishmen' is that no other policy has any prospect of success."

Mark Durkan is a northern politician who has thought carefully about how reunification might happen and the type of compromises that politicians in the south might need to make to keep unionists in the north satisfied and engaged in the reformed state. The legislature and other institutions of the state would have to change under reunification. Durkan predicts that "a new dynamic would be created by the scale of northern representation in an all-Ireland parliament as compared with Westminster. That would include a substantive unionist presence."[13]

6

SOCIAL CHANGE

THE DECLINING ROLE
OF THE CATHOLIC CHURCH

The Republic of Ireland has gone through massive social change in recent years. The effect has not merely been that Ireland has joined the mainstream of European social liberalism, but it is one of the world's more advanced nations in terms of elements of its social policy.

Historically, unionists have argued that the Catholic grip on the Irish state was itself a strong reason for them keeping their distance, given that the majority population in Northern Ireland was attached to various forms of the Protestant religion (Presbyterian, Free Presbyterian, Church of Ireland, Methodist, Baptist and others).

Unionist attitudes to the Republic of Ireland were strongly influenced by the level of influence of the Catholic Church. Ian Paisley's words may have been stronger in criticising Catholicism than were others of his faith, but the sentiments were widely shared. Paisley described Catholism as the "Seed of the serpent". He continued: "Her clothes reek of the brimstone of the pit. Her words and opinions label her the parrot of Beelzebub, her father." He also disliked what he saw as the Catholic influence on the European Union. Paisley, long an MEP, described the EU as "A beast ridden by the harlot Catholic Church."[14]

Unionists and Protestants in Northern Ireland had a point, even if the Paisley prose was excessive. The incoming Irish government of 1948 sent a message, against the advice of their officials, to the Pope that they would "repose at the feet of your holiness the assurance of our filial loyalty and our devotion to your august person".

But whatever the attitude in the past of Irish governments and today of Protestants in Northern Ireland, it is no longer possible to argue that the Catholic Church has the same influence of the Irish state as it did in the past. Leo Varadkar, the openly gay, mixed race, Taoiseach, told the Pope on his visit to Ireland that the Catholic Church had been responsible for many terrible events in Ireland and around the world. "This is a shared history of sorrow and shame", said the Taoiseach. "In place of Christian charity, forgiveness and compassion, far too often there was judgement, severity and cruelty, in particular, towards women and children and those on the margins."

In an interview preparing the way for this uncomfortable message to the Pope, Varadkar was even clearer. "I think in the past the Catholic Church had too much of a dominant place in our society," he said. "I think it still has a place in our society but not one that determines public policy or determines our laws... We do have a church/state dialogue that involves other churches as well and faiths other than Christian faiths too."[15]

It was one more step on a journey in which the Irish state has increasingly distanced itself from the Catholic Church.

DEMOGRAPHY

Ireland has benefited massive from inward investment and from inward migration. A nation that for generations sent many of its brightest and most innovative citizens abroad to earn their living, has become a receiver of migrant workers. That process went into reverse as a result of the 2008 global financial crash – as an open market economy, which failed to properly regulate its banks and property sector, Ireland was more damaged by the international recession than were most countries. Accordingly, many Irish citizens left to find work elsewhere. Since then, that process has again gone into reverse, with rapidly decreasing unemployment, rising wages and net inward migration. (Ireland returned to being a country with net inward migration in 2016.[16])

The influx of young workers from across the European Union has influenced the culture of Ireland. Dublin, Cork and Galway are open minded, youthful cities, that embrace the cultures of incomers, while retaining their Irish character. There are few of the signs of racism that inflict parts of England. Increasingly since Ireland joined the European Union in 1973, Ireland has become enthusiastically European. That European identity has marked the country as more socially progressive, less influenced by the Catholic Church, yet also increasingly different from its northern neighbour. For those citizens of Northern Ireland who are uncomfortable with the socially conservative and religiously influenced nature of its society, the Republic is now seen as a more comfortable place, ever more at ease with itself.

DIVORCE

Divorce reform was one of the early examples of the Irish state's determination to modernise institutions and policies. An initial referendum proposal to permit divorce was defeated in 1986. Ireland became the only country in Europe where divorce was not possible.[17] The then Taoiseach John Bruton argued unsuccessfully that divorce reform was necessary, to demonstrate that Ireland was a tolerant and socially advanced nation – and also to send a message to Northern Ireland that its neighbour was not under the control of the Catholic Church.[18]

A second referendum in 1995 voted, narrowly, to allow for divorce, with a carefully worded proposal that made clear that divorce could not be achieved with ease and without consideration. As a result, the Irish constitution states the dissolution of a marriage may be granted only when the couple have lived apart for four of the preceding five years, there is no reasonable prospect of reconciliation and "proper provision" has been made for the spouses and any children. One result of this is that it is likely that are at least twice as many separation agreements as there are divorces. Lawyers regard the current separation and divorce system to be "long, cumbersome and expensive".[19]

The current Programme for Government[20] includes plans for another referendum on divorce, which would further liberalise the law. Other referendums planned include potential amendments to the constitution on women's life in the home, blasphemy, reducing the voting age to 16 and extending the franchise for presidential elections to Irish citizens who live outside of the Irish state. A vote on divorce liberalisation is provisionally timetabled for June 2019.

SAME SEX MARRIAGE

In 2015, Ireland became the first country in the world to hold a referendum in which the electorate voted to legalise gay marriage. Moreover – and unlike the 1995 referendum to liberalise divorce – the vote was decisive. Some 62% of voters supported legalisation, with just 38% against. This was despite the Catholic Church campaigning for a 'no' vote. "The huge 'yes' vote marks another milestone in Ireland's journey towards a more liberal, secular society," remarked The Guardian[21]. Then Taoiseach Enda Kenny said: "With today's vote we have disclosed who we are. We are a generous, compassionate, bold and joyful people who say yes to inclusion, yes to generosity, yes to love, yes to gay marriage."[22]

REPRODUCTIVE RIGHTS

Ireland's onward journey to social liberalism was marked most clearly when in 2018 the country voted to reform the abortion law. The vote was even more strongly in favour of change than with gay marriage – 66.4% voted 'yes', against 33.6% for 'no'. Again, the Catholic Church campaigned, unsuccessful, for a 'no' vote. The result not only removed the equal right to life of the unborn, but also demonstrated that Ireland had transformed from a Catholic to a secular state.

THE CONTINUING SOCIAL CHALLENGES

While Ireland has addressed significant issues of social concern and will address others – the voting age, women's role in the home, blasphemy and presidential voting rights for the diaspora – other challenges remain without sufficient reform. The most important of these is health, which is considered in the next section. But housing, schooling and wealth distribution also remain as policy concerns for many in Northern Ireland.

HOUSING

Housing is frequently described as Ireland's biggest policy challenge. The elements are the lag in the impact of the boom and bust of the 1990s; a shortage of available property for affordable rent; excessive rental prices; a large number of mortgage borrowers who are unable to repay their mortgages and consequently a high proportion of non-performing loans on the books of mortgage lenders, which in turn inhibits their capacity to lend to new borrowers while also inhibiting borrowers' capacity to free up property by downsizing. Other problems include the shortage of property developers, with some put out of business by the 2008 crash and others engaged on lucrative contracts in GB.

"A survey carried out in Spring/Summer 2017 amongst 200 CEOs from across all industry sectors shows 84% of respondents see the lack of affordable housing as key challenge for business and the economy," reported Housing Europe. "Therefore insufficient housing supply is a concern for both its economic and social reasons as the affordability of housing is deteriorating. There were 7,941 people homeless in the week of June 19- 25th 2017 across Ireland.... The phenomenon is especially concentrated in the capital. Dublin local authority homeless services are currently managing an unprecedented demand on services."[23]

While a new policy initiative, 'Rebuilding Ireland - an Action Plan for Housing and Homelessness', was launched in July 2016, there is no confidence that the housing crisis will be resolved in the near future. The over-stretched housing market is often cited by commentators in Northern Ireland as a factor in their hostility to reunification – though it is difficult to see how the shortage of affordable housing in Dublin would immediately or significantly affect the situation in Belfast, simply because of Irish reunification. That said, it is clear that a strengthened housing policy is essential.

The combination of a booming economy, international investment, inward migration, a shortage of housing stock, enthusiastic mortgage lending and weak banking regulation proved extremely damaging to the Irish state and to mortgage borrowers when the global financial economy crashed in 2008. As yet, the Irish government has failed to address the underlying tensions that are leading to what may again be unsustainably high housing prices.

SCHOOLS

Catholic schools continue to play an important role in Ireland's education system. But the role of the church is changing and is set to change more. Ironically, the strongest indication of that new approach came in early 2018 when Taoiseach Leo Varadkar opened the first new Catholic school in Ireland for 30 years. He said that there would continue to be a place for Catholic schools within Ireland's state education system, but the role will decline.

The Taoiseach said: "There is much greater diversity now in the type of education that we offer our children and true diversity must include the Catholic religion as well... While we rightly acknowledge some of the wrongs by religious congregations in the past, we should never forget the enormous good that religious congregations have done for centuries in

Ireland. Setting up schools, hospitals, providing public welfare long before governments ever considered that to be part of their responsibility."[24]

Ireland's government has decided that as from the 2019 school year state-funded Catholic schools will be prevented from discriminating against non-Catholics who are seeking places. The Taoiseach explained: "I think for a small number of schools where there is oversubscription, it is right and proper that children would not be discriminated against based on their religion. Schools are funded by the tax payer and every tax euro is equal no matter what the religion of the parents." There will be an exemption for schools of minority faiths such as the Presbyterian Church.[25]

INCOMES AND WEALTH DISTRIBUTION

Ireland performs poorly in terms of income inequality. That relative performance was largely unchanged following the global financial crash, though incomes for the poorest 10% in society have recovered better than for the richest 10% according to the OECD.[26] Ireland remains the most unequal of the OECD's 36 member states, ahead of Greece, and with the UK in fifth place, according to Nat O'Connor of Ulster University.[27] It also has the greatest gross income inequality in the EU. O'Connor observes that Ireland's income tax system is progressive at lower ends of the income scale, but that this progressivity declines at higher income levels. The tax to GDP ratio is one of the six lowest in the EU. O'Connor adds that as an essentially low tax society, Ireland inevitably has a smaller public sector and higher costs of living than other, higher taxed, states. Ireland's cost of living is 20% above the EU average.

Taxation of income on the two sides of the border is significantly different. This is a factor that could influence many people's attitudes to reunification. UK rates as at April 2018 were: income up to £11,850 is tax free; taxed at 20% from £11,851 to £46,350; 40% from £46,351 to £150,000; and 45% for income above £150,000.[28] In the Republic, income up €34,550 is taxed at 20%, above that at 40%. (This is for a single person without children.) The Universal Social Charge also applies on income above €13,000. But a range of tax credits mitigate the total tax liability. Because of the complexity of the Republic's tax system it is difficult to compare the results of the two systems. Broadly, low paid workers pay less income tax in the Republic than in the UK because of the impact of the Republic's tax credits, while middle and higher income individuals pay more tax.[29] The Republic's basic corporate tax rate is 12.5%, compared to the UK's main rate of 19%.

The state pension is higher in the Republic than in the UK, but begins a year later. The UK's state pension is not only the lowest in the EU, it is also the lowest in the developed world.[30] However, it would be for negotiation whether Northern Ireland residents would receive a UK state pension or the more generous Republic of Ireland's state pension.

Social Justice Ireland has expressed concern at low pay in the private sector and argues that the national minimum wage is 20% below a living wage.[31]

7

A FREE HEALTHCARE SERVICE
- A PRECONDITION FOR REUNIFICATION

Health service reform is essential in both Irish jurisdictions. Neither service achieves excellence: in fact, neither service at present is adequate. Waiting lists and waiting times are too long in the north, while the lack of universal provision at primary level and the need for private insurance cover makes the southern system unattractive to voters in the north and is a major cause of discontent in the south.

The establishment of a free at point of need healthcare system in the Republic of Ireland offers benefits for the south and is probably essential to win support in the north for a united Ireland. This might be modelled on the National Health Service – but an effective NHS, not the one in Northern Ireland that is currently blighted by inadequate funding, the failure to implement reform as spelt out by the Bengoa report[32] (and other studies) and with excessive waiting lists and waiting times.

There is already best practice health provision in some disciplines, involving cross-border co-operation and treatment. Examples include the cancer care centre at Derry's Altnagelvin Hospital, which provides services to patients on both sides of the border, cuts the need for cancer patients in Donegal to travel to Dublin for treatment and provides a cost-efficient service for NI taxpayers through economies of scale by expanding the number of patients treated, whose costs are covered by the Irish state.

Another example is the co-operation between ambulance services in the border areas. DUP former health minister Edwin Poots agreed with the Irish government that children's heart surgery would be carried out in Dublin[33], preventing the need for children to fly to Britain for surgery, or providing an expensive service in NI that would have meant surgeons less familiar with procedures carrying out operations. Heart surgery is an example of treatment that is more safely conducted by those surgeons who conduct the procedure most frequently.

EXPERT ANALYSIS

Professor Jim Dornan was the person who initially proposed Dublin's children's cardiac surgery unit becoming an all-island facility to enable higher quality specialist services to be provided. He strongly supports a further move towards an integrated all-island health service in Ireland. Professor Dornan says: "I believe Ireland is a Goldilocks country – just the right size for an integrated health service with good infrastructure that allows super and regional centres of excellence. The joint population is perfect!"

He adds: "It is the core culture of the National Health Service that it belongs to those who deliver, and those who require, its services. It is the aim of every country to provide an efficient, caring, effective, healthcare infrastructure, and a body of well trained, vocationally driven personnel who help set the clinical agenda for a proactive sensitive management team to implement.

"Ireland wants and needs to have its people as healthy as possible at all times, and for its citizens to increasingly take personal responsibility for same. This should be encouraged from the early years and throughout life. At the same time introduction of the New Zealand 'No fault compensation' concept should be considered as this is the best alternative for those who deserve same, while at the same time removes much of the fear element from the healthcare provider.

"The new efficient, ambitious, responsive Health Service should seriously consider introducing, at the top, the concept of a lay chief executive and team, instead of a health minister, thus removing decision making from the political arena. I believe that while all essential healthcare should be free at the point of delivery, there are many successful models worldwide where socialised medicine can work to the benefit of all while working in a hand in glove relationship with the private sector, without hypocrisy or rancour.

"We live in exciting times where medical knowledge is doubling every seventy days, while at the same time patient expectations are rising, and so adequate funding commensurate with the countries' economy must be provided by direct and fearless taxation, the amount of which is in keeping with the wishes of the electorate."

PROF JIM DORNAN MD (HONS) FRCOG FRCPI
Chair Health & Life Sciences UU
Emeritus Chair Fetal Medicine QUB

Dr Desmond Brown also favours an integrated all-island health service. He says: "There are benefits of scale, firstly. Northern Ireland is too small an entity to provide all the specialist services, integrated procurement and land/air transport. We are already co-operating with the Republic as well as the rest of the UK in complex surgery and cancer therapy, successfully. We are operating as part of the European community in that patients from Northern Ireland can receive treatment in the Republic or any other country in the EU, paid for by their health service, and that is happening now, to alleviate waiting times."

DR DESMOND BROWN
Former paediatric consultant for the NHS in NI and
Ontario Regional Neonatal Service

THE DECLINE OF THE ROLE OF THE CATHOLIC CHURCH IN THE REPUBLIC

It would be unacceptable to most residents of the north to have a health system dominated by provision involving the Catholic Church. But despite the history, reform of the south's healthcare system is underway.

The Catholic Church's involvement in health and schools provision in Ireland dates back to the 19th Century, at a time when the state provided neither. The role of the Catholic Church was the greater in Ireland, because such a high percentage of the population were of the Catholic faith and the British state pre-independence was regarded as being unfavourably disposed to Catholics. Following independence, the weak Eire state had insufficient funds to provide core health services and schools, and was happy to rely on the Catholic Church. In turn, the Church was able to arrange services at cheap cost through the use of members of the religious orders and volunteers.[34]

As well as being engaged in the provision of health services, the Catholic Church was also dominant in determining policy. In 1950, proposed government legislation on adoption, social welfare and support for pregnant women were all abandoned – in effect by instruction of Catholic bishops. Although the Irish constitution was secular, government was very definitely Catholic. Bishops could, and did, instruct government ministers on what to do, and more specifically what not to do.

When health minister Noel Browne attempted to introduce a Mother and Child Service that would provide free maternity care for mothers and free health care to children under 16 he was forced to leave government. The measures were abandoned. The Catholic Church had effectively vetoed them, in part because of fears that gynaecological care of pregnant women might have been provided by non-Catholics – which might have led to women being advised to have terminations, or supported in having them.

Then Taoiseach John Costello supported the Catholic bishops against his own health minister, Browne. Costello told the Dáil of his meeting with the Archbishop of Dublin, John Charles McQuaid. "I asked His Grace would he permit me to try to adjust the matter with my colleague [Browne]. His Grace readily gave me that assignment and that authority." In a subsequent letter to Browne, Costello wrote: "You are not entitled to describe your scheme as government policy and you must not so describe it hereafter unless and until you have satisfied the [Catholic] hierarchy." The Catholic Church's veto over Irish health policy was proven.[35]

HEALTHCARE REFORM IN IRELAND

Inequality in the delivery of healthcare in Ireland is a serious problem, which is related to the system operating in the Republic. "Those with a lower social position are more likely to report unmet health care needs, as well as unmet medical examination and treatment needs," reported NERI. "When looking at the situation for Ireland as a whole it is clear that cost and waiting lists were the key reasons for unmet health care need, these issues are more problematic for those with lower income and lower levels of education attainment."[36]

A committee of the Oireachtas, chaired by Roisin Shortall TD, proposed in its SláinteCare report[37] fundamental reform of healthcare provision in Ireland. The adoption of the committee's recommendations would be the basis for meeting many of the concerns of residents in Northern Ireland in relation to healthcare provision in a reunified Ireland. The committee reported in May 2017 and made far reaching and comprehensive proposals for the reform of healthcare in Ireland. The key challenge, said the committee, was to achieve a universal single tier health service in which patients are treated on a basis of need, not their ability to pay.[38]

The starting point for the committee's approach was to recognise the serious weaknesses in the existing system in the Republic. These included the severe pressures on the current provision; unacceptable waiting times for public patients; and poor outcomes in relation to the cost of the provision. (Ireland spends around 40% more than the EU per capita average on healthcare, yet is the only country in Western Europe not to have a universal primary healthcare system. About 70% of Ireland's healthcare spending is publicly funded, which is much less than the EU average.[39]) The report explained: "A key cause of Ireland's relatively high spending may well be its emphasis on an expensive model of healthcare delivery. Too much emphasis has been placed on providing care in acute settings without appropriate use of, and investment in, primary and social care. Moving to a better model of service delivery should prove more efficient and eventually cheaper though investment is needed to help reform."[40] Scotland's health care system was cited as a best practice model by many stakeholders.[41]

The committee concluded that there needs to be a universal single tier service in which patients are treated on the basis of health need rather than on ability to pay. It also concluded that better health outcomes and value for money can be achieved by re-orientating the model of care towards primary and community care.

Healthcare cannot be provided on the cheap and the committee was clear that resource allocation must increase, proposing an additional €233m over the period 2017 to 2027. The preferred funding design model[42] is through solidarity funding. Budget pooling and re-fencing were suggested.[43] The establishment of a national health fund was proposed, to be funded from general tax revenues and the earmarking of some taxes, levies or charges into a single national health fund (NHF). This would help build more transparency, sustainability and independence into health funding.

A ten-year budgeted cost to expand entitlement was developed and outlined[44], as was the methodology used to arrive at the budgeted figures. The allocation and source of funds to enable SláinteCare and cost areas of implementation were identified. Charges for healthcare should be removed or reduced, said the committee, including the removal in full of charges for emergency care by year eight.

The funding for improved healthcare assumes allocation from

Ireland's 'fiscal space'. It should be noted that this would be a competing demand for tax revenues with any continuing subvention for Northern Ireland that might be needed. Funding would also need to come from higher tax revenues, not all of which are likely to be generated from increased economic activity. As NERI observes, while many individuals would need to pay more in tax, this will be partially or fully offset for many by lower private insurance premiums.[45]

The committee also recommended[46] the development and utilisation of a geographic allocation formula to ensure the equitable allocation of resources based on both population characteristics and activity levels. An integrated module of health workforce planning (WFP) was proposed. It was recommended that hospitals' consultants and NCHDs should be accountable to the hospital groups, rather than to individual hospitals. This would help meet the medical staffing needs of smaller hospitals.

The committee had a vision for integrated care[47] and aimed[48] to propose a system that delivered the triple aims of healthcare: to improve care, improve health and reduce costs. The committee recommended[49] that integrated care in Ireland be delivered through three integrated streams: system strengthening, service co-ordination and network building. In addition, the committee proposed clear steps for the phasing and implementation of integrated care[50]. This involved the prioritisation of the resourcing of critical patient-care and management systems: eHealth; financial management; workforce planning (including performance management and career advancement); health service performance and accountability systems; and health status and outcomes data integration.

Primary care should be made universal and its services expanded, including through the provision of community-based diagnostics, with more of the care currently provided by the acute sector being transferred to primary care providers. New GP contracts were outlined[51].

It was recognised that private health care provides a crucial role in any health care system, as do voluntary providers. However, the committee recommended[52] that private patients no longer be treated in public hospitals and a fund be established to replace the €649m (2016 figure) private income that would be lost. These reforms need to be backed by new legislation, additional funding, political consensus and structural change, said the committee.

The committee learned lessons from Sweden[53], which was one of the first to introduce waiting time guarantees with strong sanctions and economic incentives, with the ability for patients to exercise their right to use an alternative provider. These solutions should be built-in, in a manner which is compatible with each citizen's electronic health record. The committee also recommended[54] horizontal integration across community hospitals and ambulance services, with seamless care between communities and hospital services.

Other weaknesses in the current provision need to be addressed, said the committee. These include social care, with the provision made available of universal palliative care, additional services for people with disabilities and improved mental healthcare. There should be an expansion in the public psychology service. Strategies for mental health[55] and the importance of a rights-based approach to health care[56] were identified. Dentistry services also need to be made more widely available[57].

The development of an effective eHealth strategy for Ireland is essential, as it provides lower cost, more accessible and more intelligent healthcare. Plans for eHealth development are already underway throughout the Irish health system.[58]

It was recognised that it was necessary to conduct further reviews of the strategies and models in use internationally to identify and implement best practice in medicines management, including evaluation, procurement and usage; international collaboration and active co-operation with other EU member states, to share information and utilise all opportunities for joint negotiation, in particular through our membership of the European single market; and of the appropriate oversight and audit of the prescribing and dispensing patterns, including through the use of Primary Care Reimbursement Service (PCRS) data where available.

A proposed implementation body was recommended[59] to be set up and new structures and timetable and legislation were outlined for the implantation of SláinteCare. The committee proposed a ten year plan for health service reform, urging a political consensus be formed behind its recommendations.

OVERALL ASSESSMENT OF SLÁINTECARE

The proposals represent a plan for a modern European health system with a clear and implementable plan which, if properly funded as indicated, would lead to achieving the goal of "a universal single tier health service were patients are treated on the basis of need other than the ability to pay".

These proposals provide the basis for not only producing a modern, effective and cost efficient health service for the Republic, but also for a more effective and cost efficient health service for the whole island of Ireland. These would achieve economies of scale, which would also achieve improved access to specialist services for patients across the island of Ireland. Moving towards an integrated health service does not need to be dependent on Irish reunification. It is a sensible move which should be the basis of reform of the NHS in the north, as well as more radical change in the south. The outcome would be a health service that is not only better and more widely available to people in the south, it would also be better than the service currently available via the NHS in the north.

IRISH GOVERNMENT'S SUPPORT FOR SLÁINTECARE

The Irish government is supporting the adoption of SláinteCare, not just in principle, but also financially. Fine Gael health minister Simon Harris has endorsed the proposals, though without any clear timetable for implementation.[60] Fianna Fail has also explained its support for SláinteCare.[61]

Finance minister Pascal Donohue has approved funding for the early implementation stages of SláinteCare and gave these comments as part of his 2019 Budget.[62]

"This year I will allocate an additional €700m by way of a supplementary estimate, bringing the total additional 2018 investment to €1.2bn. I am announcing a further increase of €1.05bn in health funding for 2019. This brings the health budget to €17bn. Taken together, the additional investment in health in the last two years comes to €2.25bn or an increase of 15%. This is the highest level of health investment in the history of the state. The allocation I am announcing today will facilitate a range of additional services including initiatives proposed under Sláintecare."

THE NEED FOR REFORM IN NORTHERN IRELAND

A series of reviews of the operations of the NHS in Northern Ireland have concluded that the service is not meeting current demand and requires significant reform. The Bengoa review explained: "Across the system, there has been a broad consensus among those the [Bengoa review] panel has spoken to that there is a need for transformational change in the way services are delivered and the way our system is organised. It is important to fully understand the nature of the challenges and demands that health and social care services face, and also the reasons why the model that is currently in place is outdated and is not the one that Northern Ireland needs."[63]

The review considered best practice examples of where reform has taken place, including amalgamating service provision on a cross border basis.

"Cross-Jurisdictional Level – Children's Congenital Heart Surgery"

In recent years the regional Paediatric Congenital Cardiac Surgical (PCCS) Service, provided by the Belfast Trust, developed vulnerability in its surgical service due to new international safety and quality standards which could not be met because of our relatively small population size. As evidenced by clinical reviews neither surgical centre (Belfast or Dublin) had been delivering a service which meets current international standards of both institutional case volume and consultant staffing: the service in Belfast did not meet the surgical case volume threshold, and the Dublin service has a medical staffing level in both intensive care and cardiology that is significantly lower than in comparably sized UK and European centres. By December 2014 Belfast could not continue to provide an emergency and elective surgical service, and by April all interventional cardiology procedures ceased in Belfast (as these require the presence of a surgeon). An International Working Group (IWG), led by Dr John Mayer from Boston Children's Hospital recommended the establishment of an all-island congenital heart disease (CHD) service, with a single surgical centre in Dublin capable of meeting international standards for surgical practice volumes, supported by specialist cardiology hubs in Belfast and other locations. The 'hub and spoke' network would involve all stakeholder groups including patient representative organisations in its governance structure, and be supported by enhanced telemedicine links, improved transportation, and a clinical research programme.

"The all-island CHD Network was established in April 2015, following a public consultation on the recommendations of the expert group. In endorsing the IWG's recommendations, commitment was also given to the development of a specialist Children's Heart Centre in Belfast, enhancing existing facilities at the Clark Clinic within the current footprint of the Royal Belfast Hospital for Sick Children and making it fit for purpose until the new Children's hospital opens in 2021/22. This will secure the role of RBHSC as an integral part of the in the all-island 'hub and spoke' network, functioning as a 'Level 2' cardiology centre, i.e. providing the full range of non-surgical care required by CHD patients until they are ready to transition into the adult service. The all-island

CHD Network involves the two Health Departments, commissioners, service providers (management and clinicians) and patient representatives in a collaborative non-statutory structure to deliver an all-island CHD Service in line with the relevant legal and accountability arrangements that apply in each jurisdiction."[64]

CONSENSUS

There is a consensus across the medical profession in Ireland that there is a need for fundamental reform for health care provision in both Northern Ireland and in the Republic. A large number of those medical professionals in both jurisdictions believe that this might be best achieved through a merger of the two systems, bringing together the best of each and achieving economies of scale that enable a significant improvement in specialist services and broadening access to primary health care.

8

AN ALL-ISLAND ECONOMY

A TALE OF TWO ECONOMIES

David McWilliams gained respect as the best known Irish economist to predict the global economic crash of 2007/8 and who warned that Irish property prices had become a bubble. He might now be the economist who reads it correctly about the financial benefit of Irish reunification. McWilliams examined the issue in some detail - and very few economists have done so - after Ireland's foreign affairs minister Simon Coveney said he would like to see a united Ireland in his lifetime.

McWilliams presented key economic statistics illustrating that since partition, the economies of the Republic and Northern Ireland have increasingly diverged.[65] The northern economy that was strong in 1922, is now weak. The southern economy that was weak in 1922, is now strong. "The union with Britain has been an economic calamity for Northern Ireland," said McWilliams. "All the people have suffered, Catholic and Protestant, unionist and nationalist."

He continued: "In 1920, 80% of the industrial output of the entire island came from the three counties around Belfast. Belfast was the biggest city in Ireland in 1911, larger than Dublin, and was home to Ireland's innovation and technology. At partition the North was industrial and rich, the South agricultural and poor....

"The Republic's economy is [now] four times larger, generated by a work force that is only two and a half times bigger. The Republic's industrial output is today 10 times that of the North. Exports from the

Republic are 17 times greater than those from Northern Ireland, and average income per head in the Republic, at €39,873, dwarfs the €23,700 across the Border.... Dublin is three times bigger than Belfast, far more cosmopolitan and home to hundreds of international companies."

McWilliams also pointed out – in an article published in the Belfast Telegraph - that while a peace dividend was expected for Northern Ireland, it was actually delivered for the Republic. "Since the Good Friday Agreement, American corporations alone have invested close to $400bn (£312bn) in the Republic," he explained."[66]

Economies are often compared on the basis of GDP per person. In the case of the Republic, GDP per head is a flawed measure owing to the movement of capital and the transfer of asset ownership by multinationals domiciled in Ireland for tax reasons.[67] Ireland's Central Statistics Office is experimenting with the GNI measurement in place of GDP. EY's Neil Gibson observes that using this measures also demonstrates better economic performance in the Republic. "Expressed per head, GNI is more than 10% higher [in RoI] than GDP per head in the UK and roughly 45% higher than GDP per head in NI."[68]

GVA (gross value added) is regarded by many economists as a more relevant measure.[69] In 2014 – before the latest Irish economic acceleration - GVA per capita in the Republic was €38,100[70]. By comparison in Northern Ireland it was £18,682[71], the third lowest of any UK region.[72] Using current exchange rates that equates to less than €22,000, or about 57% of the figure in the Republic. Average full time income per head in the Republic in 2016 was £40,403 (€45,611[73]), compared to £25,999[74] in Northern Ireland. In other words, a worker in the Republic is typically paid half as much again as someone working in Northern Ireland.

However, disposable income is comparable in real terms north and south. In 2015, average household income by purchasing power parity was €13,300, in the border, midlands and western region of Ireland and €15,500, in the southern and eastern region (containing Dublin and Cork). In Northern Ireland in 2015, the figure was €15,400 per household. In 2007, before the crash, the figures were €13,700 in the border, midlands and western region, €15,800 in the southern and eastern region and €14,500 in Northern Ireland. Pay figures in the north are to a significant extent flattered by higher average pay in the public sector (but the same is true in RoI, albeit with a proportionately smaller public sector). In 2017, median average weekly pay in Northern Ireland was £501 (£26,052 per year). There is a significant variation between average full time pay in the public and private sectors. In 2017, median average private sector weekly pay was £446, compared to £623 in the public sector.[75] That equates to £23,192 in the private sector, or £32,396 in the public sector.

In the Republic, in 2017, mean[76] average income was €734.60 in Q4 2017, while in the public sector it was €946.55.[77] This was a 28.9% higher pay in the public sector than the average pay in both public and private sectors. The Republic was severely damaged by the global financial crisis of 2008, but since then average real incomes have grown much faster in the Republic than in the UK – and Northern Ireland lags the UK as a whole.

In mid 2018, the unemployment rate in NI was officially 3.8%, which – unusually and amazingly – was below the UK rate of 4.0%. (Figures as at end of June 2018, published in August 2018.[78]) In the Republic at the same point it was 5.8%.[79]

Superficially, the unemployment position seems much better in Northern Ireland than in the Republic. But economic inactivity is very high in Northern Ireland. Consequently, the employment rate is a more useful indicator of the state of the labour market. Northern Ireland's employment rate at May 2018 was 69.8%[80]; while the Republic's was 68.5% in mid 2018.[81] While the official unemployment situation is worse in the Republic, the real level of unemployment, after taking into account economic inactivity, is only marginally different.

The Republic's economy is much more globally focused than is Northern Ireland's. Based on statistics from the International Monetary Fund's World Economic Outlook Database, Ireland's total Gross Domestic Product amounted to $324.3bn as of November 2016. Therefore, exports accounted for 39.5% of total Irish economic output.[82]

For Northern Ireland, exports accounted for 20% of output (as measured by GVA), which is above the UK level of 17%. The Republic of Ireland is NI's largest export destination (31% by value), with the EU as a whole (excluding GB) responsible for 55% (by value) of NI's exports.[83] Northern Ireland's export levels are likely to be significantly diminished by Brexit, whatever form it takes. The Republic's global focus makes it much more vulnerable than the UK to global shocks, but much better positioned to take advantage of global growth.

Irish economic policy in the 1990s was the basis for remarkable growth. "EU membership, and the single market programme of the late 1980s and early 1990s, were essential in allowing Ireland to finally reap the full economic rewards of its independence," wrote Kevin O'Rourke in a 2016 Oxford University paper. "The policy mix that we adopted is well known: a low corporation tax and other incentives for inward investment, including investment in education and infrastructure."[84] The author adds that social partnership, wage restraint, stable industrial relations, political independence and EU membership were all part of an attractive policy environment.

"Underpinning everything was two crucial factors: our political independence, which allowed us to adopt a policy mix well suited to our own circumstances; and our membership of the European single market, without which none of this would have worked."[85] While economic policy was subject to some major errors (such as weak banking regulation), which exposed Ireland disproportionately to the global crash of 2008, it is clear that Ireland had a fundamentally strong economy – strong enough, in fact, to deal with the punishing regime of bailing-out its failed banking system.

WIDENING ECONOMIC GAP

EY's Economic Eye study for summer 2018[86] reported that while economic growth in the Republic in 2017 was 7.8%, in Northern Ireland it was a mere 1.6%. Its prediction for 2018 was for GDP growth in the south of 4.9%, compared to 1.1% in the north. Worse still, an earlier EY Economic Eye[87] predicted that while the Republic will generate an additional 91,000 jobs by 2020 compared to 2016, the north will lose 3,500 jobs.

According to EY, factors behind the strong Irish performance include being well positioned to benefit from global economic growth – which Northern Ireland may not be. Mike McKerr, EY Ireland's managing partner, commented: "The RoI economy is generating significant momentum suggesting some resilience to Brexit, though it differs across sectors and locations. The retail and consumer sector appears to face a profoundly challenging time in Northern Ireland."

EY's Winter 2017 Economic Eye reported: "The headline data suggests an increasing divergence in economic fortunes across the island. The Republic of Ireland sits atop the European growth charts, while Northern Ireland is closer to the bottom."

The Central Bank of Ireland reported in its 2018 Q3 economic bulletin that: "The Irish economy continues to grow at a robust pace, supported by the strength of activity on the domestic side of the economy and a favourable international growth environment."[88] Pay is also rising, with a 3.3% increase in average weekly pay in the second quarter of 2018 compared to a year earlier.[89] The strength of the labour market is also reflected in strong inward migration figures, with nearly 20,000 more people at work in the Republic now than before the global financial crisis.[90] [91]

"Looking ahead, the outlook remains positive and the Central Bank's central forecast is that the economy will grow at a relatively strong pace in 2018, with a slight moderation in growth in prospect next year," added the Central Bank's forecast. "Notwithstanding this gradual slowing, underlying domestic demand is projected to grow by 4.4% this year and 4.1% in 2019."[92] Unemployment is predicted to fall marginally, to 5.6% in 2018 and 4.8% in 2019, with an additional 99,000 persons forecast to be in work by the end of 2019.[93]

By contrast, the CBI in Northern Ireland has warned of the risk of recession, reflecting low levels of optimism in the context of Brexit and the lack of government in Northern Ireland – which is holding back infrastructure investment.[94]

HOW THE DIFFERENCE IS EXPLAINED

There are a variety of reasons for the difference in economic performance since partition. Clearly, the Troubles was one factor. This damaged the economy of Northern Ireland and of border counties in the Republic, particularly Donegal. The Good Friday Agreement failed to deliver the 'peace dividend' at the levels expected.

Partition has also been damaging to the whole of Ireland, especially the border region. The economic damage to border areas has eased, but remains noticeable. Average disposable incomes in Donegal and the north east border areas rose from 75.6% of the Irish national average in 1973 to 92.5% in 1994, and in 2002 it was around 90%.[95] The most recent statistics published by the EU on average regional pay shows the Republic's border, midland and western region still has average pay below that of the southern region.[96] It is to be hoped that reunification would increase the focus of the new state on Donegal and other border areas – not least because road transport connections from Dublin to Donegal would no longer need to cross an international boundary.

The continuing situation is well described by the Irish Borderlands website, published by Queen Mary college, part of the University of London[97]. "The borderlands of Northern Ireland and Ireland are amongst the most disadvantaged and deprived areas of the island. Though places near the border's eastern region, including the cities of Newry in Northern Ireland and Dundalk in Ireland, have recently grown in prosperity as part of the Belfast-Dublin axis of development, most of the borderlands were badly affected by the Troubles and continue to suffer the significant negative economic and social effects of the border. As in other contexts, the creation of a border in an area previously traversed by long-standing and multiple networks – familial, social, economic – dramatically distorted or destroyed these existing links and interconnections. While some pre-partition social networks continued on a cross-border regional or all-island basis, for many people old patterns of family connections and friendships were broken, severely curtailed, or a struggle to maintain."

A more fundamental economic reason over the longer-term for the difference in performance relates to the different sectoral focus of the two economies. At partition, Northern Ireland was dependent on heavy engineering, such as shipbuilding, and on shirt making. These industries have been badly affected by globalisation and Northern Ireland has been only partially successful in stimulating replacement industrial sectors.

The UK economy has refocused away from manufacturing to the service economy. This has tended to increase inequality and the wealth divide in the UK. London has prospered, while regions that have traditionally been more dependent on manufacturing have suffered.[98] The 'Great Recession' increased regional disparities, with London recovering more strongly and more quickly than have other, weaker, regions.[99]

The restrictive nature of devolution for Northern Ireland limited the regional assembly's capacity to develop its own industrial strategy that reflected its distinctive needs – recovering from the collapse of the shipbuilding and textiles sectors – and the challenge of geographical marginalisation. "The inability of the new Northern administration to deviate in any significant way at all from UK-wide policy simply reflected the extremely limited scope for local autonomy that was provided for in the 1920 Government of Ireland Act under which its local parliament (Stormont) operated," argued John Bradley in his important analysis 'The History of Economic Development in Ireland, North and South'.[100]

Northern Ireland's economic decline resulted from the lack of international investment because of the Troubles and the "serious crisis" in economic policy in the north.[101] Northern Ireland "tracked" the manufacturing decline of the UK as a whole, but without generating a new private services sector to compensate, asserted Bradley.[102]

Northern Ireland has compensated by becoming increasingly reliant on the public sector for employment, with a big growth in public sector employment between the mid 1960s to the late 1980s.[103] With Northern Ireland having a higher corporation tax rate than the south, the north's inward investment has tended towards low cost support services, rather than profit centres. Multinationals have tended to prefer to locate profit centres in the Republic, where they can pay a significantly lower rate of corporation tax. (It should be noted that the Republic's corporation tax advantage is being challenged both by proposals from the European Commission and US tax reforms, which make Irish tax residency less attractive for corporations. Despite this, the Republic is still very attractive from a corporate tax perspective.)

The Republic has benefited from IDA Ireland (formerly known as the Industrial Development Agency), which has been assisted by the low rate of corporation tax to be much more effective than the north's Invest NI in attracting foreign direct investment (FDI). But multinationals have been attracted to Ireland not just because of the tax rate: other factors include a highly skilled and motivated labour market; a welcoming culture for migrant workers and managers; the English language (an important advantage with regards to attracting US investment destined for the EU); and substantial investment in infrastructure (particularly in the big cities). It is important to note that another important factor has been IDA's ability to influence government policy, for example to improve roads infrastructure to assist with attacting FDI to regions away from Dublin.

The perception in Northern Ireland is that Invest NI does not have the same policy influence, with the result that there are high levels of unemployment and lower levels of inward investment in the north west of NI. This policy was reinforced by the Barnett review of economic policy which endorsed "the importance of government policy not seeking to unduly influence the location of FDI within NI".[104]

"RoI in recent decades has performed well globally in attracting inflows of foreign direct investment (FDI), despite challenging economic circumstances," reported a Northern Ireland Assembly research paper.[105] It added that FDI was disproportionately attracted to Dublin and Cork, with less investment attracted to other cities and regions. However, following the global crash, IDA was given a target of 50% of new investment being located outside these two cities.

In 2017, IDA Ireland attracted 111 new foreign investors, as well as working with 76 existing investors who expanded their operations in the course of the year. This created almost 20,000 (19,851) new jobs from FDI companies, with the result that 210,443 people in the Republic are employed by overseas businesses, with the support of IDA.[106] By comparison, Invest NI 'promoted' 5,600 new jobs in the 2016/17 year. 'Promoted' is not the same thing as created, as it includes jobs that have been promised by inward investors, but not yet delivered – some of which may take several years to arrive, and some of which will never be delivered. It attracted 22 new investors into NI during the year.[107] There is a clear and strong difference in performance between the two agencies. However, this may be less to do with the competence of Invest NI and more to do with more effective policy levers being applied in the Republic.

The Republic has been clever in its targeting of growth sectors, particularly those that prosper in a globalised economy. RoI has an open economy, from which it is easy to trade internationally. As a committed member of the European Union, the Republic has benefited from investment from both within and outside the EU. Ireland is recognised by investors from countries outside the EU – particular the United States, but also other countries such as Israel – as an excellent bridgehead into the EU. But the second largest foreign investment source is Germany[108], above the UK's level of investment and helps explain why 'Irexit' has little traction in Ireland. Dublin's International Financial Services Centre has been a major success, attracting banks, accountancy firms and fund managers, and acting as the major global base for various niche activities, such as aircraft leasing.

Current factors affecting RoI growth include: Brexit relocations from London; continuing foreign direct investment from the United States, despite US tax cuts; the effectiveness of IDA Ireland; the low corporation tax rate; the strong skills base; Ireland's ability to attract global talent, both Irish returners and others, because of strength of economy, the character of existing FDI, and increasingly socially liberal society; a focus on key sectors, including IT, pharmaceuticals and activities with profit centres; Ireland's integration into the global economy; and the attractiveness of Ireland to the financial services sector – the speaking of English, tax rates, an even lower effective tax rate, and the strong cluster of professional firms specialising in the financial services sector that are based in Dublin's International Financial Services Centre. Ireland's political stability, compared to the systemic instability in Northern Ireland, is another positive.

There are a number of variations in terms of public policy between the two jurisdictions. The Republic of Ireland's corporation tax rate is 12.5% (some corporations have been able to avoid even this). Northern Ireland is subject to the UK rate, which is currently 19%. While outline agreement between the main parties was achieved for Northern Ireland to match the Republic's rate, the failure of those parties to also achieve a sustainable and continuing administration meant the lower rate has not been implemented.

There is a greater focus on skills and qualifications in the Republic than in Northern Ireland. While 45% of young people in the Republic complete their education with a degree or higher, this is true of only about 31% in Northern Ireland.[109] More than a third of Northern Ireland school leavers who go on to university do so in Great Britain, most of whom do not return to work in Northern Ireland.[110] While 26% of Northern Ireland's adult working age population are graduates, the figure is over 35% in Dublin and Cork.[111] Both the Republic and Northern Ireland suffer from a problem of too many adults being without basic skills.

PRODUCTIVITY

According to PwC, the Republic of Ireland is around 60% more productive than is Northern Ireland.[112] Productivity across the UK has been a challenge in recent years, holding back recovery after the Great Recession. But productivity is a significantly greater challenge in Northern Ireland than in Great Britain. "Whilst productivity has slowed at national [UK] level and the UK has lost some ground relative to competitor nations, the gap between NI and the UK average has been persistent and widening for many years despite being the target of a number of economic strategies," observed Ulster University.[113] It added: "GVA per head in NI is only 75% of the GB average. This means that there is a 25% productivity gap between the GB and NI."[114]

Moreover, there is a worrying variation in productivity levels within Northern Ireland, which points to policy neglect in terms of the sub-regions within the north. The UK has the fifth weakest productivity within the G7[115], with Northern Ireland some 17% below the UK average[116], but Belfast is 12% below UK average, the west and south of Northern Ireland 20% below the UK average and the north of Northern Ireland about 23% below the UK average.[117]

There are a number of factors that dictate the level of economic productivity, most of which come down to policy decisions, including investment. The UK's 'productivity handbook' named five factors as being critical in determining productivity growth: these are investment, innovation, skills, enterprise and competition.[118]

In terms of private sector investment, this has lagged because Northern Ireland has been insufficiently attractive to international investment, while also not producing enough high margin indigenous businesses. In part, this is a circular argument – investment is not attracted to locations that have the reputation and reality of suffering from low productivity. Moreover, footloose capital is typically attracted to a low tax jurisdiction, other factors being equal.

The lack of public sector investment is arguably at least equally relevant in the case of Northern Ireland. It has a significant infrastructure deficit, for example in terms of roads, rail and digital connectivity (see below). This damages productivity as it takes longer to get goods to market, for executives to travel to meetings and for commuters to get to work. The lack of fast broadband in rural areas of

Northern Ireland is another major impediment.

The absence of innovation is itself the result of a combination of factors: the lack of foreign direct investment; the limited tax incentives to locate state-of-the-art private sector R&D facilities in Northern Ireland; the small size of the university sector (the number of Northern Ireland school leavers going on to university elsewhere would be sufficient to populate an additional university in Northern Ireland[119]); and the absence of a more competitive commercial environment (see below).

Northern Ireland lacks skills at all levels: it has too few graduates; it has a shortage of technical vocational skills; and it has too many people without basic skills. "The skills deficit in NI is sizeable and enduring and the most worrying statistic is for those with no level 1 National Vocational Qualifications. NVQ stratifies a range of qualifications ranging from GCSEs to trade apprenticeships and University degrees. In 2015, 16% of 16 to 64 year olds did not have a level 1 NVQ. To have less than a level 1 NVQ means less than 5 GCSEs at A-C grade."[120]

With a sub-par economy, people with the best skills tend to be attracted elsewhere, leaving behind those with inadequate skills – for whom other places are not welcoming. In effect, the market works in ways that leave the least skilled people in Northern Ireland, without offering sufficient incentives to retain or attract those with the highest skills. With private sector pay lagging behind that of the public sector, more than half of graduates in Northern Ireland are attracted to work in the public sector.[121]

The issue of enterprise is a regular bug-bear for Northern Ireland. Too few new businesses are created in Northern Ireland and too few of those that are set-up survive. Northern Ireland has the weakest entrepreneurial environment of the UK's four nations and the lowest rate of new business start-ups. "The distribution of TEA [Total early-stage Entrepreneurial Activity - the intention to start a business] rates in 2015 was similar across the home nations: England at 7.2%, Wales at 6.8%, Scotland at 6.7% and Northern Ireland at 5.4%".[122] "Northern Ireland is the one UK region where businesses births and deaths (registration and deregistration) were almost equal, at roughly 9% of registered businesses in 2014; the UK business birth rate in 2013 was 14.1% and the death rate was 9.7%. Since 2009, Northern Ireland has been persistently below the rest of the UK in terms of the net change in the number of business registrations, with an annual decline in the total number of businesses registered."[123]

One of the major challenges for the Northern Ireland economy is the lack of progression from small to large. If more small firms could become large, then Northern Ireland would have a bigger and more competitive economy. Instead, the indigenous economy is dominated by small firms. "Small and medium-sized companies and self-employed people, together, provide 75% of employment, 75% of turnover and 81% of GVA in NI's private sector. Furthermore, SMEs actually employ more people than NI's large companies and the public sector combined."[124]

It can be argued that these problems relate to a significant extent to the small size of Northern Ireland, with a population of just 1.8 million people and a land border to the south and a sea border to the east. There are cost barriers to competing with Great Britain and trade barriers – some regulations and differences in tax regimes – with the Republic of Ireland. Becoming a more integrated part of a larger all-island economy can be expected to generate a more competitive environment, strengthening productivity in the process.

Policy-based causes of weak productivity would presumably be addressed by government and corrected post-reunification. This would lead to a gradual levelling-out of economic performance between the Republic and Northern Ireland.

John FitzGerald has examined the issue of weak NI productivity in an article in the Irish Times. He explained: "The low investment rate in the North has been translated into a steady fall in labour productivity, measured as output per person employed, relative to the UK average. Between 2000 and 2014, the North's productivity fell from 93% of the UK average to 80%. What makes that even worse is that the UK's productivity has itself been declining over the last decade relative to European Union partners. So the North has been experiencing a falling share of a falling index."[125]

Politics (and economics) is often about making assumptions. The assumption of this author is that following an extended period of austerity in GB and a one-off deal from the UK government involving a £1bn additional fiscal transfer to NI, that there will be a point where UK government generosity towards NI recedes. At some time it is likely that NI will suffer GB levels of reduced public spending. Moreover, Brexit will inevitably lead to a significant change in economic focus, which will have a major impact on NI. There needs to be a rise in NI levels of productivity, which is likely to involve a further reduction in the public sector headcount. So the conversation should not be about comparing a united Ireland with the status quo – rather comparing two alternative future visions of where NI society moves towards.

THE INFRASTRUCTURE DEFICIT

Northern Ireland's infrastructure is inadequate and is a key factor in its weak productivity. Evidence for this is clear: long commuting times in Belfast, limited motorway and rail connectivity, poor road connections in the North West and large parts of the rural areas without fast broadband speeds.

The House of Commons Northern Ireland Affairs Select Committee warned in 2017 that "Without urgent investment in Northern Ireland's energy infrastructure, the industry is not confident it will be able to keep the lights on after 2021."[126]

In summer 2016, a joint report from the CBI and Ibec argued for improved infrastructure to support the all-island economy. Its priority was a major upgrade to create a modern, all-island, road network that connected all key urban centres, including the link between Dublin and the north west of Ireland, Sprucefield by-pass to improve the connection between Dublin and Belfast and an upgrade between Sligo and Letterkenny. It argued that these improvements would "embed peace and prosperity" and help "to bring economic opportunities and prosperity to every region, locality and community."[127]

Northern Ireland's Investment Strategy plans for a capital spend on infrastructure projects of £8.2bn for the five year period 2015/16 to 2020/21. Priorities include £1.2bn for road projects (including the Belfast to Derry, and Derry to Dublin connections, Belfast's York Street interchange and the Belfast to Larne road); £1.9bn for healthcare buildings (hospitals, primary care, etc); £1.2bn on schools; £1bn on water and waste water; and £855m on housing.[128]

This can be contrasted with the much more ambitious €116bn infrastructure investment plan[129] for the next decade published by the Irish government. This potentially provides one of the EU's highest levels of publicly funded infrastructure investment. While it is true that there are also contributions from motorists to road funding through tolls in the Republic, it may be that northern motorists and businesses might be willing to pay tolls if these led to higher investment and shorter journey times.

However, planned investment is insufficient to address Northern Ireland's existing infrastructure deficit. Northern Ireland's weak infrastructure is, in part, the result of inadequate investment during direct rule years: it can therefore be argued that the UK government should contribute to addressing this deficit.

NORTHERN IRELAND'S TRADING RELATIONSHIP WITH GREAT BRITAIN

In 2016, 15% of Northern Irish sales and exports of goods and services beyond its own geographical borders went to the Republic of Ireland.[130] This had a value of around £4.3bn[131] and represented 5% of total NI production[132]. The value of trade to the north from RoI was worth much less to the Irish economy, at around £1.3bn.[133] Northern Ireland's exports of goods to the whole EU, including RoI, was about £7.8bn in 2016.[134] Northern Ireland's sales to GB were of much greater value, at about £15bn. This compares to internal sales within Northern Ireland, of about

£50bn. However, much of Northern Ireland's sales to GB contain materials or ingredients sourced from the Republic, via integrated supply chains: Brexit therefore threatens the basis of much of NI trade with GB.[135] Moreover, one and a half times more Northern Ireland businesses sell to the Republic than sell to GB.[136] Exports are more important to NI than to GB: they constitute 20% of NI output, compared to 17% of the UK as a whole.[137] These factors demonstrate the need for NI businesses to be able to trade freely with both GB and RoI, both post Brexit and post reunification. Reduced trade either west to east or north to south would be extremely negative for NI. Brexit negotiators must ensure the undamaged continuation of both.

The big questions, then, are: would Northern Ireland's sales to GB significantly fall if Northern Ireland left the UK and became part of a united Ireland?; would sales to RoI and the rest of the EU increase at a scale to compensate for that?; and would a gradual transfer from being part of the UK to being part of a United Ireland mitigate the negative impact on sales to GB? It is important that an economic plan be drawn up to consider how traders in Northern Ireland could either continue to trade at the same level with GB after reunification, or else replace that trade with the EU. It is important that NI maintains a close relationship with GB, whether or not it becomes part of a united Ireland. That could best be achieved by avoiding tariffs and border controls and to support trade to continue to be conducted in sterling.

According to analysis from the Northern Ireland Assembly[138] the top five exported commodity groups from Northern Ireland in 2017 were machinery and transport (£2.88bn, 33.7%); chemicals (£1.42bn, 16.7%); food and live animals (£1.34bn, 15.7%); other manufactured items (£1.31bn, 15.3%); and manufactured goods (£0.76bn, 8.9%). It is impossible to predict to what extent these goods exports to GB would continue following a united Ireland. There would be a particular challenge for Northern Ireland's manufacturing sector, which sells more goods into GB than it does into Northern Ireland, RoI and the rest of the EU combined.[139]

9

THE BREXIT EFFECT

At the time of writing, a few months before the UK leaves the EU, it was unclear what deal, if any, would emerge from negotiations between the UK government and the European Commission. It was also unclear whether any negotiated deal could produce a majority in the House of Commons or the support of the other 27 EU member states. Uncertainty rules.

A bad Brexit outcome would be damaging to both Northern Ireland and the Republic of Ireland. While the Irish Republic will also be damaged by Brexit, the impact is likely to be less than on the UK, in particular on weaker UK regions (especially Northern Ireland). Issues affecting the Republic included transport access to markets and suppliers based in continental Europe, as well as in the UK.

The UK's Treasury predicted that a 'no deal' outcome would negatively impact Northern Ireland along with the north east of England worse than other UK regions.[140] According to Sky News[141], unpublished Treasury analysis concluded that without a deal with the EU, Northern Ireland's economy would be 12% smaller than it would have been without Brexit; with a hard Brexit deal, it will be 8% smaller; and with a soft Brexit deal (retaining membership of the customs union through EFTA, for example) it will be 2.5% smaller. In published correspondence, the Treasury said, in relation to the UK as a whole: "This January [2018] provisional analysis estimated that in a no deal/WTO scenario GDP would be 7.7% lower (range 5.0%-10.3%) [over a 15 year period] relative to a status quo baseline [without Brexit]".[142]

According to the European Parliament: "Northern Ireland is the part of the UK most distinctly affected by Brexit."[143] It pointed out: "Growth in exports to EU countries from Northern Ireland has considerably outpaced that to non-EU countries in recent years and amounted to £3.63bn in 2014, compared to £2.53bn of non-EU exports.... The importance of Northern Ireland's current tariff-free and quota-free trade relationship with the Irish Republic is apparent, with 34% of Northern Ireland's EU exports heading there (21% of the region's total exports). This makes Ireland the largest market for Northern Irish exports. More broadly, the majority of Northern Ireland's exports (57%) head to the EU."

The UFU reports that "87% of Northern Ireland's total farming incomes comes from the Single Farm Payment."[144] Northern Ireland's farmers receive one of the highest payments-per-hectare annual awards in the EU and 9% of the UK's total allocation of EU pillar payments.[145]

Northern Ireland's GVA for 2016 was £37.2bn.[146] If a 'soft Brexit' outcome is negotiated, the likely economic impact would be a loss of potential economic output of £930m a year, based on the lowest Treasury assessment. The potential loss would be £1.1bn, using the projections from the European Parliament's report. The economic impact of a 'hard Brexit' that hits potential output by 8% would be £3bn (£1,600 per person) and a no deal situation would reduce the potential size of the economy by 12%, which would be £4.5bn (nearly £2,500 per person). If we assume (as a rough guide) a reduction in employment pro rata for the reduction in the potential size of the economy, that would mean 67,000 fewer jobs under the 8% impact scenario, or more than 100,000 jobs fewer under the 12% scenario. (There were 837,000 people employed in Northern Ireland as at November 2016.[147])

The CBI in Northern Ireland is particularly worried about the impact of migration restrictions following Brexit. It argues that Northern Ireland is the UK region most dependent on inward migration for its labour market: its demography is of an ageing population, with a large number of the most skilled and mobile individuals moving abroad for better career prospects. Modelling conducted by the CBI concluded that a 50%

reduction in EU inward migration would decrease Northern Ireland's potential GDP by 5.3% by 2041, but that if the reduction was not just of EU inward migration but also a global reduction, the impact would be a 9.1% reduction in potential GDP. "Under these same scenarios, the working age population in Northern Ireland would shrink by around 6% and 8% respectively," said the CBI. The impact would be greatest in some of the border areas, particularly Derry & Strabane and Armagh City, Craigavon & Banbridge.[148]

THE AGRI-FOOD SECTOR

The agri-food sector is particularly important for the Northern Ireland economy – and is especially at risk from Brexit. There are more than 29,000 farmers in Northern Ireland, who receive more in EU Common Agriculture Policy payments than from market prices.[149] "Currently, 87% of Northern Ireland's total farming incomes comes from the Single Farm Payment", says the UFU.[150] Total income from farming in 2016 was £244m.[151]

Brexit represents a threat on three levels to the farming sector. Firstly, there is the potential loss of labour, with many food producers reliant on workers from elsewhere in the EU, with a shortage of local labour willing to do this work. Secondly, there has been a significant increase in cross-border commercial operations in recent years, as agricultural and food producing organisations achieve economies of scale through cross-border mergers, such as Lakeland and Fane Valley. Food processing, in part as a result of this, can involve crossing the border repeatedly. Thirdly, there are fears that the replacement of the Common Agricultural Policy is likely to lead to a loss of support to farmers generally[152] and to Northern Ireland farms in particular[153].

Brexit is a potential disaster for Northern Ireland's farmers and food producers, who are dependent on EU financial support.

Northern Ireland receives funding from a number of EU funding schemes[154]. These comprise the European Regional Development Fund, the European Social fund, the Regional Development Fund, Interreg, the

Common Agricultural Policy, the Common Fisheries Policy and the Peace programme (currently Peace IV, scheduled to complete in 2020). Once NI leaves the EU it will be unable to receive several of these, though Peace funding is likely to continue if a negotiated Brexit outcome is achieved. Should NI become part of a united Ireland, it will again be eligible to receive EU funds.

In total, Northern Ireland is due to receive €3.5bn in EU funding between 2014 and 2020. It is unclear whether all schemes currently funded by the EU that will not continue post-Brexit will be replaced by the UK government. There has been speculation that Northern Ireland will receive a smaller share of CAP funding in future which is relative to its population share of the UK, 3%, rather than its current 9% of the UK allocation of CAP. If that were to happen, it would be an annual loss of around half a billion euro coming into NI.

Farmers in Northern Ireland are particularly dependent on EU subsidies. The Northern Ireland Assembly explained: "... the [EU's] Basic Payment Scheme currently accounts for 103% of the average Farm Business Income in Northern Ireland. The ending of such support could threaten the viability of many farms, particularly if there was neither a replacement or gradual wind down to enable readjustment. The income shock of removal of direct support could see a significant drop in the number of farmers. This could well create a rural unemployment impact that would extend beyond the farm gate as many rural shops and businesses indirectly benefit from farmers spending their BPS. There could also be a large scale abandonment of land if farmers go out of business and dereliction could also be a problem due to a lack of incentives to maintain environmental standards. A drop in the number of farmers could theoretically benefit those who managed to continue to operate as prices might rise for certain produce providing demand exceeded supply and farms might be able to expand if land became cheaper/available. This could make remaining businesses more profitable/efficient and potentially lead to employment generation."[155]

However, as the Assembly report adds, there is no certainty that the EU will continue with the CAP scheme, not least because of its cost. One possible outcome, the report suggests, is that any policy on continued direct payments will be devolved to the national administrations, but, if so, it is unclear whether this would be fully funded.[156]

It is worth noting that it is predicted that the UK's farming sector will shrink by perhaps around 15% as a result of Brexit. One academic, Dr. Michael Wallace of Newcastle University, has projected that "close to 100%" of UK farms are likely to be worse off.[157]

Some of the strongest advocates of Brexit – Economists for Brexit/Economists for Free Trade, who have close links with some parts of the Conservative Party – argue that abolition of CAP is one of the most important aspects of Brexit. "The CAP system leads to high food prices for UK consumers, increases inflation and reduces disposable income, which otherwise would boost consumer spending and thus the economy. Moreover, it artificially inflates agricultural land values, which further increases the cost of food and has wide knock-on effects to prices across the entire economy."[158] Under policies influenced by them, there would be significant reductions in support payments for produce, as well as lower land values. This would be a double whammy for Northern Ireland farmers, though potentially cheaper land for housing development. It is likely that agri-food exports from NI to GB will anyway decline as a result of Brexit, with perhaps more food imported from around the world to take advantage of weaker regulation and greater economies of scale achieved in countries such as the United States, Argentina and Brazil.

UK government reform to CAP will reduce support payments to farmers, disproportionately affecting Northern Ireland. "Leaving the European Union and the CAP will give us the opportunity for fundamental reform," says a government consultation paper on farming support payments in England. "We want a more dynamic, more self-reliant agriculture industry as we continue to compete internationally, supplying products of the highest standards to the domestic market and increasing exports."[159] It adds: "We believe this is a vision that could work for the whole of the UK but we recognise that devolution provides each administration with the powers to decide its own priorities." But not, presumably, with devolved funding at current levels after 2020. "We therefore propose to further reduce and phase out Direct Payments in England completely by the end of the 'agricultural transition' period, which will last a number of years beyond the implementation period."

It is also worth noting the sub-regional impact of CAP payments within Northern Ireland. "£266.3m was paid out in single farm payments and £83.1m in rural development funding. ... Beneficiaries based in the Enniskillen area received the largest amount of CAP funding - £38.9m in total. This was followed by the Omagh area (£33.3m) and then the Ballymena area (£27.3m). The top ten town/city areas each received over £10m in EU payments – Enniskillen, Omagh, Ballymena, Newry, Dungannon, Armagh, Derry/Londonderry, Craigavon, Coleraine and Magherafelt. The majority of these towns/cities are west of Northern Ireland which is an area that historically struggles to attract as much funding as the east."[160]

10

FAILED DEVOLUTION

Devolution has differed in Northern Ireland from Scotland and Wales. Firstly, the law making devolved to the three devolved nations differ in each instance. Secondly, Scotland and Wales were in essence functioning places prior to devolution – and they continued to function effectively after devolution. For both Scotland and Wales devolution meant giving local politicians the power to make careful adjustments to existing programmes and spending priorities that reflected policies their parties had been elected to implement.

In Northern Ireland, the situation has been substantially different. Northern Ireland was not operating effectively prior to devolution. It was in crisis – a crisis in the sense that the Troubles had afflicted civil society and government for 35 years. And the sectarianisation of government meant layers of excessive spending – the security forces were too big for a peaceful society and spending on schools, housing and community facilities were bloated because of service duplication. The Alliance Party has estimated the cost of failing to integrate service provision at around £1bn a year.[161]

Add to these inherent and inherited problems the strong mutual antipathy felt by members of some of the different parties, it was perhaps simply too much to expect a Northern Ireland Executive to emerge that could undertake fundamental reform of society and its governmental institutions. Whether that is the case or not, the truth is that devolved government has failed to achieve these reforms. The obvious example is with the NHS, where Northern Ireland has the longest waiting times and per capita waiting lists of any UK region.[162] [163]

Devolution has also been disappointing for Northern Ireland in terms of its economic impact. When the GFA was signed in April 1998, the NI employment rate was 65.4%. By the end of 2017 it had improved modestly to 68.7%. Compare that to the UK situation. At the time of the GFA the UK employment rate was 71.7%, which increased to 75.6% by the end of last year. In 1998, NI lagged the UK employment rate by 6.3%. At the end of last year, it lagged it by 6.9%. So despite devolved government, the employment rate differential has widened.

This performance differential has been noted by the Resolution Foundation.[164] A comparison in the reduction in the proportion of households where no one is working shows that Northern Ireland dramatically underperformed every other UK region. In the period between 1996/99 and June 2018, there was a 9.7% reduction in Northern Ireland households in which no one was working. This was the weakest improvement of any UK region, about half as good as the next weakest (the East Midlands, where the improvement was 18.7%). The UK average was an improvement of 27.4%, while in Inner London the improvement was 49.3%. This represents a startling economic and social underperformance in Northern Ireland compared to every other UK region.

This has created a situation where Northern Ireland has the highest proportion of any UK region of households in which no one is working. In NI, it is 21.1%; the next worst is the north east, where it is 18.6%; the UK average is 14.4%; and the best performance is recorded in outer London, where it is 10.3%.

The failure of devolution to improve the fundamental strength of Northern Ireland's economy has been noted by commentators. John FitzGerald observed: "The history of the Northern economy, since the Good Friday agreement, is that there has been little progress in transforming it into a self-sufficient economy, which could sustain the standard of living currently supported through transfers from London."[165]

Overall, devolution in Northern Ireland has been a failure in terms of economic development policy and outcomes. As John Simpson observes, looking at what has happened since the Good Friday Agreement and based on what has happened elsewhere, Northern Ireland should now be in a much better position. "UK and Irish comparators suggest that average personal incomes might be about 6%-8% higher, employment could be 5% higher and net emigration several thousand lower."[166]

As well as reflecting a failure in government leadership within Northern Ireland, there is also a clear failure in leadership by the UK government, spanning several political generations. This has resulted in a very high level of inequality within the UK. (Former Greek finance minister Yanis Varoufakis argues that the pro-Brexit referendum outcome was a result of the failure of English regional economic policy.[167]) Inner London is the richest region in Northern Europe; by contrast Northern Ireland is the eighth poorest region in Northern Europe – all ten poorest regions are in the UK.[168]

There has also been a massive failure by government – under direct rule and in pre- and post-Troubles devolved administration – to address sub-regional requirements. There is a large variation in productivity rates across Northern Ireland (see above), which reflects the lack of investment in skills and infrastructure outside of Belfast. It is further reflected in the substantial variation in employment rates across Northern Ireland. As at mid 2018, while the UK's employment rate was 75.6% and the Northern Ireland employment was 69.7%; in the north west (the Derry City & Strabane Council area) the rate was 56.8%. This was almost certainly the lowest employment rate for any sub-region in the UK.

11
THE HUEBNER ANALYSIS: MODELLING IRISH UNIFICATION

The Huebner report has made an important contribution to the analysis of the potential economic benefits of Irish reunification. It was widely criticised at the time of publication, primarily because although it was written by independent and respected academics, it was commissioned in the United States by supporters of Irish republicanism. However, this does not undermine the conclusions, given the author's credibility.

Huebner's report concluded that using its assumptions (which predate the Brexit vote), unification could benefit people across the island of Ireland by €1,497 per year in the year of implementation, rising to €2,810 per person per year within seven years of implementation. Most of the financial benefits would be felt in the north.[169]

The report's reasoning included:

1   Tax harmonisation at RoI levels will be beneficial to the north. Lowering corporation tax levels to those of the Republic is likely to generate higher levels of foreign direct investment. (However, a working NI Assembly could choose to do that without reunification).

2   Diminished trade barriers will increase trade. (Clearly this

is correct in terms of trade between NI and RoI and will be even more true post-Brexit.)

3   Adoption of the euro in the north would be beneficial, because the pound was over-valued at the time of the report's publication. (Given sterling's devaluation means that the pound is no longer obviously over-valued against the euro, this point is out of date. Sterling is now competitive with the euro.)

4   Productivity improvements. (It is reasonable to assume that if NI adopts the industrial strategy of the south then it will – over time – move towards the productivity levels of the south. But this could take decades. 27 years after German reunification, productivity remains lower in the east than in the west and wages remain lower. Achieving economic benefits from unification is a slow process.)

5   Political union will lead to rationalisation of the public sector in the north.

6   Fiscal transfers will become the responsibility of the Republic, not the UK.

One key finding of the report is how important borders are, in terms of disrupting trade. It explains: "Numerous studies done in a variety of settings (the US and Canada, among Canadian provinces) demonstrate that 'borders matter' to a much greater degree than most observers would expect." The return of a hard border on the island will obviously be detrimental. The most aggressive unification scenario in the report estimates a boost in all-island GDP of €35.6bn over eight years with the north benefiting significantly more than the south.

The report concluded: "The model... suggests unification will raise GDP in NI by €2.1bn to €2.6bn in the year the policy is implemented, depending on the extent to which NI government expenditure is cut and the amount of FDI attracted by the new tax regime. These gains could accumulate to as much as €25.3bn in the first eight years following unification. GDP in the ROI could rise by €30m to €152m in the year of policy implementation, again subject to the same assumptions. Across the first eight years of unification, GDP gains in the ROI could rise from €10.3bn to €18.5bn. In total, Irish unification could boost all-island GDP in the first eight years by as much as €35.6bn."

As the authors of the report point out, in the case of German unification the smaller partner - East Germany - benefited the most. However, it should be noted that the benefits spread slowly – reunified Germany is still far from being an equal society, or having equivalent economic output. It should be noted that west and east Germany remain different places in terms of economic performance, social relations and political outlook.[170] Despite this, reunification can be regarded as having been a success. And it is reasonable to say that the task of German reunification was more challenging than would be the case of reuniting Ireland. The economic systems on both sides of the Irish border are broadly similar, though performing at different levels. In Germany, one jurisdiction had free market capitalism, while the other had state capitalism – involving subsidies for state run factories, for example. Since reunification, East German productivity has risen from 73% of the German average in 2000 to almost 80% by 2014.[171] This is significant, if slow, progress. Reintegration of divided countries is not easy.

12

COULD THE REPUBLIC AFFORD NORTHERN IRELAND?

I t is commonly said that Northern Ireland is subsidised to the tune of around £10bn a year by the UK government. But that depends on how the figure is calculated. One calculation takes into account Northern Ireland's share of total UK government expenditure – the armed services, debt interest and central government administration in London, for example, which are collectively termed the 'non-identifiable' items. A very different figure is arrived at if only the direct costs of Northern Ireland are taken into account.

The former Northern Ireland Department of Finance and Personnel estimated total revenues for Northern Ireland of £14.9bn in the 2013/14 year, compared to £24.1bn in public spending. On this basis a calculation of a subvention of £9.2bn is arrived at for that year. However, NERI – the Nevin Economic Research Institute – estimated that if various non-Northern Ireland items of expenditure are removed from the figures then the actual subvention for the year was around £5.2bn (around €5.9bn).

THE FISCAL IMPLICATIONS OF IRISH UNITY

By *Tom Healy* of NERI[172]

In the past, the union between Northern Ireland and Great Britain was defended on economic as well as other grounds on the basis of the claimed benefits flowing from integration into the much larger British and commonwealth or imperial markets as well as the economic and political backstop of a strong united kingdom. The demise of manufacturing, in Northern Ireland, and the huge shifts in global power and trade position of the UK means that these claimed benefits are less obvious today than was the case 100 or even 50 years ago. From being a basket case economy southern Ireland showed remarkable dynamism and growth potential from the 1960s onwards and especially during the period of rapid growth in 1993-2007. By the turn of this century the south had overtaken the UK and Northern Ireland in terms of GDP per capita.

Advocates of a united Ireland frequently use economic arguments to make the case for unity on the grounds that an island economy would benefit from integration and lowering of costs and inefficiencies associated with two separate jurisdictions and currency areas, etc. There is some truth in this claim (although difficult to assess because it is a very hypothetical one). It is also the case that Northern Ireland benefits from integration in to a single large UK market while both Ireland the UK benefit from partial integration into a much larger market of 500 million in the European Union.

Two key inter-related questions arise in debates about these matters:

1 The extent of fiscal transfer from the UK centre to Northern Ireland
2 The hypothetical 'cost' to the southern Irish taxpayer of a united Ireland.

The 'Net Fiscal Transfer' is the estimated value of the difference between, on the one hand, what Northern Ireland contributes by way of total taxes and government revenue collected (most of which is remitted to the central UK authorities), and on the other, what is spent by public authorities for and by and in Northern Ireland. The reference to 'for' and 'by' and 'in' is important!

The Department of Finance Personnel (DFP) report Net Fiscal Balance Report, 2012-13 and 2013-14 provides an estimate of the overall position with regard to 'for', 'by' and 'in' as well as splitting out the 'in' by means of 'identifiable' public spending in Northern Ireland. The methodology used in the DFP report is that used by the Scottish Government in its annual publication 'Government Expenditure and Revenue in Scotland' (GERS). Using this methodology 'non-identifiable' expenditure refers to spending undertaken at UK level and which cannot be decomposed on an individual regional level. Key examples would include the service of national debt or the cost of the UK military (except where, perhaps, components of military spending can be identified with a particular region). Strictly speaking, spending 'for' a region such as Northern Ireland may take place at central (Whitehall) level in government departments dealing directly with payments, receipts or administration of Northern Ireland.

Non-Identifiable Expenditure is considered to occur on behalf of the UK as a whole and cannot be decomposed on an individual country or regional basis. It is standard practice in studies of inter-regional government transfers to apportion or estimate part of national 'overheads' to a specific region even when these costs cannot be directly associated with the region. The rationale is that all regions, without exception, are implicated in the cost or revenue. In the case of regional transfers among the regions of the Republic of Ireland a similar type of apportioning exercise is undertaken by researchers.

In summary, the DFP report estimates a total government revenue of £14.9bn in 2013-14 compared to a total of £24.1bn in public spending. However, when 'non-identifiable' spending is excluded total spending came to £20.1bn. So, depending on which measure of spending is used, the 'net fiscal deficit', in 2013-14 was £9.2bn or £5.2bn.

An important fact not considered in the current debates is that the share of total government revenue in total regional income (GDP if you like), in Northern Ireland, is approximately 50%. This is hugely above what it is in the Republic (35%) and in the rest of the UK. In area of health spending less than 10% of households in Northern Ireland purchase private health insurance compared to a corresponding figure of nearly 50% in the Republic. The difference is explained in three letters: NHS. Would Northern Ireland taxpayers be willing to pay less tax to have a three-tier health service such as is the case in the Republic? Perhaps this question should have been asked in the recent RTE/BBC survey?

The methodology used in the DFP report has been the subject of controversy. Apart from the question of 'non-identifiable' expenditure there have been questions about what parts of administrative spending 'for Northern Ireland' by Departments located in Britain should be included as well as estimations of tax receipts from households and corporations. It is suggested, for example, that the DFP report under-estimates Northern Ireland taxes paid by UK companies headquartered in Britain but sourced in Northern Ireland. While this is a possibility it is unlikely to be that large. The DFP report, on page 46, provides a summary of the various official data sources used in estimating revenue streams. The report authors are careful to point out the following:

Particular caution should be used in relation to individual components of the fiscal balance as many revenue streams have been estimated and are not true values.

Were an alternative approach to be taken using HM Revenue Commissioner estimations total government revenue for Northern Ireland would be £14.3bn instead of £14.9bn per DFP report – widening the estimated fiscal deficit to £9.8bn.

Whatever about revenue estimate differences, is it legitimate to include non-identifiable spending in regional estimates of fiscal transfer? I believe that the answer is yes. It is a standard part of regional economic analysis and it reflects the extent to which transfers act to reduce inequalities by region. This is the pattern in many countries where regional disparities exist such as in Italy, Germany, France and even the Republic of Ireland (difficult as it is to measure regional transfers).

So much for net fiscal transfers. Estimation of how much a united

Ireland would cost the southern taxpayer (and not forgetting about the Northern taxpayer) is quite another matter. And this is where the story gets even more complicated!

If, hypothetically, in the year 2115 Northern Ireland were to leave the UK and be united with what is now the 26 counties to form a single all-island state what might the implications be for fiscal policy in Ireland?

To keep things simple for now let's assume no change in GDP or its components for both parts of Ireland. (It may be objected that a united Ireland would release new possibilities and economic activity so as to boost productivity and government revenues. This might or might not be the case and the burden of proof rests with those making these claims.) On the basis of no policy change and no change to GDP, it is clear that a unification of Ireland would entail some additional financial cost to the government of a united Ireland compared to the current situation. After all Northern Ireland is the poorest region of the UK and if there is a transfer to it such as there is to Northern England regions then a transfer to the North of Ireland post-reunification is not unlikely.

That part of the net fiscal transfer from London to Belfast which relates to 'identifiable' spending (approximately £5bn or €6bn) would be required to maintain Northern Ireland public services at the current 2015 levels. But, the story does not end there. Living standards (and social transfer payments) in the Republic are significantly higher than they are in Northern Ireland so that there would have to be a process of adjustment over a number of years to bring the north up to the standards of the south. This would be analogous to the post-reunification German solidarity tax of 5-7% on all incomes (the size of an Irish unity solidarity tax may not be as big as that).

What of the 'non-identifiable' spending? There is a point that this spending would not be relevant particularly if any reunification scenario Northern Ireland's notional share of UK national debt were written off under the new arrangements. Instead of sharing in the UK national debt, Northern Ireland would now share in Irish national debt and the annual cost of servicing it (as well as Irish national administrative overheads). In this case, southern taxpayer may not necessarily have to pay more by way of tax. The national debt (and its annual servicing cost) would simply be shared among 32 counties rather than 26. However, given the 'unknown unknowns' Irish national debt might be higher than would otherwise be the case because of reunification due to lingering structural features of the Northern Ireland economy and society. And security costs might be higher than might otherwise be the case were there an absence of near universal enthusiasm for a united Ireland among both communities in Northern Ireland (a simple voting majority within Northern Ireland would not be enough to ensure enduring political stability and near universal buy-in by [both] sides of the community).

The harsh reality so often avoided – North and South – is that unless we wish to turn Ireland into a prototype of a low-tax and low-public spend economy such as prevails in the USA then taxes will have to increase especially in the South where a rising and ageing population will require additional taxes to pay for public services in education and health. This is why a policy of cutting income taxes in the South is socially inequitable, fiscally irresponsible and economically damaging and not supported by any solid empirical evidence (see a working paper by my colleague Dr Tom Mc Donnell – Cultivating Long-run Economic Growth in the Republic of Ireland).

The first question to be considered is not where to draw political lines on maps but what quality of society and economy we wish to establish in Ireland and in Britain. And it should not be forgotten that integration of the island economy especially in areas such as energy, health and agri-business does not necessarily require Northern Ireland's exit from the UK. However, a Brexit could change all that quickly. Beware of black swans.

It can be safely concluded that the south as well as the north have a lot of work to do to transform their respective economies and societies to make unity attractive if such were to be seriously proposed. However, at the end of the day, these matters will be resolved on the basis of political choices by all of the peoples of this island reflecting historical and social ties and loyalties.

Tom Healy is director of the Nevin Economic Research Institute

NORTHERN IRELAND'S PUBLIC SECTOR

There are around 396,100 public servants in the Republic of Ireland,[173] 8.4% of the population. There are around 206,430 public servants in Northern Ireland,[174] 11% of the population. This compares to 8% for the whole of the UK. (The statistics for RoI comprise the civil service, defence, the garda, education, regional bodies, health and semi-state companies. For Northern Ireland, the figure comprises employees of NI central government, arm's length government bodies; UK central government employees based in Northern Ireland, local government and public corporations.)

More than 50,000 jobs would go if the public sector in the north were reduced in proportionate size to that of the Republic. Average weekly public sector pay in Northern Ireland is £623[175]: this suggests the potential annual cost savings of a loss of 50,000 public sector jobs in Northern Ireland is around £1.6bn per annum in wages, plus £145m in national insurance contributions. In addition, workplace accommodation costs would be saved. However, the loss of these jobs would potentially create additional welfare benefits costs and loss of spending in the wider economy, unless equivalent jobs could be created in the private sector. In recent years across the UK, the loss of public sector jobs has been less than the creation of new jobs in the private sector – but these have typically been at lower rates of pay and a high proportion of them have been self-employed or otherwise insecure.

While the direct cost savings to public sector bodies would potentially be in excess of £1.7bn a year, the net benefit to public expenditure would be significantly less than this. It should also be recognised that the projected savings assume that the public sector in Northern Ireland has the capacity to improve efficiency and also that the security situation is normalised, with no increase in politically-motivated violence before or after Irish reunification.

THE THUMANN REPORT

In July 2018, a report was published examining in more detail the potential subvention required for Northern Ireland in the event of Irish reunification. 'Northern Ireland's Income and Expenditure in a Reunification scenario'[176] was researched by Gunther Thumann, who had been senior economist at the German Desk for the International Monetary Fund during German reunification, and Senator Mark Daly, for the Oireachtas Joint Committee on the Implementation of the Good Friday Agreement.

This report drew on earlier research (including some contained in this book), in particular that commissioned by Congressman Brendan Boyle from the United States Congressional Research Service. This earlier research examined the income and expenditure for Northern Ireland with a view to producing an independent assessment of the actual subvention of Northern Ireland in the event of Irish reunification. Thumann broke down Northern Ireland's expenditure into identifiable expenditure, non-identifiable expenditure and accounting adjustment. The non-identifiable expenditure included £2.9bn towards UK-wide defence and debt interest.

Northern Ireland's fiscal accounts are adjusted to bring them into line with the statistical requirements for UK government accounts. Thumann calculated that £1.1bn of the accounting adjustments would not apply to Northern Ireland in a reunification scenario. (The adjustments include the Bank of England Asset Purchase Facility, Central Government Capital Consumption, VAT refunds and imputed subsidies.)

Thumann and Daly concluded that identifiable expenditure in Northern Ireland's 2012-13 Social Protection budget included pensions accounting for £2.8bn. "These would initially be the responsibility of the British Government as the pension liability was accrued while Northern Ireland was part of the United Kingdom," they explained.

An additional £1.7bn of annual reductions could be deducted from the subvention in the public service employment in the north could be brought down to a proportionate level with that in the Republic.

The authors concluded: "Taking the above adjustments and savings into account the cumulative figure is £8.5bn. With the reported deficit for Northern Ireland at £9.2bn therefore the current income and expenditure figure for Northern Ireland comes near a balanced budget in a reunification scenario. This is of course before taking into account the likely potential for growth in Northern Ireland following unification as happened in East Germany following its reunification and to eastern European countries on their accession to the EU."

They add: "While this £9.2bn figure is a statistical measure of the 2013-2014 fiscal situation in Northern Ireland (as part of the United Kingdom) it would not be an adequate measure for the fiscal balance of Northern Ireland under a unification scenario with the Republic of Ireland. First, the Boyle report data contain expenditure items which would not be present under a unification scenario. Second, the fiscal situation of Northern Ireland will depend on the economic situation and the tax and expenditure structure at the time of unification, which could be quite different from that in 2013/14. Third, the future fiscal situation of Northern Ireland will reflect policies adopted in the context of unification."

Thumann points out that while German reunification has not achieved economic equality, it has created a substantial improvement in the east German economic situation. He wrote: "East German productivity rose rapidly in the first ten years of unification – from about 45% of the West German level in 1991 to about 75% in 2001. East German productivity was still a little below 80% of West German productivity in 2013. In 2013, disposable household income per capita in East Germany had reached €17,614, equivalent to 83% of the West German level; the gap had narrowed considerable from the 61% figure measured in 1991."

IRELAND'S BUDGETARY POSITION

In the 2017 year, Ireland's expenditure was €77.5bn, with revenues of €76.5bn – a deficit of €1bn[177], or close to a balanced budget. Huebner's analysis predicts that tax revenues in both of what are currently two jurisdictions would rise following reunification. Whether Ireland can afford to absorb the fiscal situation of the north therefore depends on whether tax revenues can increase, but also on the true size of the subvention in Northern Ireland. It might also depend on whether the UK government would co-operate.

THE ATTITUDE OF THE BRITISH

Any discussion of the prospect of a United Ireland needs to take into consideration the attitude of the population of Great Britain. Given the absence of concern for the impact of Brexit on Northern Ireland within the Brexit debate (other than within Northern Ireland), it seems reasonable to infer that it is not a major issue for large numbers of people in Britain. Indeed a post-Brexit opinion poll suggests that the majority of the British population are indifferent to Northern Ireland.

An opinion poll survey conducted in January 2018 asked a sample of voters whether an independent trade policy was more or less important than "protecting the soft Irish border". Across the UK there was a 58% preference for an independent trade policy, compared to just 28% who prioritise a soft Irish border. Northern Ireland was the only UK region where a soft border was regarded as more important than an independent trade policy.[178]

This provides clear evidence that the interests of Northern Ireland are not prominent in the minds of the British electorate. If those British voters were given a choice as to whether to retain NI within the UK, the answer might well depend on the issue of cost.

While there is a debate over the real level of UK government subvention to Northern Ireland, there is clarity over the much higher public spending in Northern Ireland. Public spending per head of population in Northern Ireland was £11,042, which is 21% above the UK average, and the highest amount of any UK region. In the south east of England it was £8,111. Much of this difference comes down to the much higher size of the public sector in Northern Ireland.

A major restructuring of Northern Ireland in terms of its public spending position within the UK seems likely, or inevitable, even if it continues within the UK. The removal of Northern Ireland as a cost to the UK would be welcomed by large numbers of taxpayers in GB, particularly in England. It seems very likely that whatever happens politically that there must be substantial reform in the coming years to the Northern Ireland economy and structure of public service delivery.

13
A BILL OF RIGHTS

The Belfast Agreement (Good Friday Agreement) makes several references to a potential Bill of Rights for Northern Ireland, as well as compliance with the European Convention on Human Rights. It should be noted that prime minister Theresa May has in the past indicated her desire to remove the UK from the remit of the ECHR, but has since pulled back from that aspiration.

The Belfast Agreement says:

"The new Northern Ireland Human Rights Commission will be invited to consult and to advise on the scope for defining, in Westminster legislation, rights supplementary to those in the European Convention on Human Rights, to reflect the particular circumstances of Northern Ireland, drawing as appropriate on international instruments and experience. These additional rights to reflect the principles of mutual respect for the identity and ethos of both communities and parity of esteem, and - taken together with the ECHR - to constitute a Bill of Rights for Northern Ireland. Among the issues for consideration by the Commission will be: • the formulation of a general obligation on government and public bodies fully to respect, on the basis of equality of treatment, the identity and ethos of both communities in Northern Ireland; and • a clear formulation of the rights not to be discriminated against and to equality of opportunity in both the public and private sectors."

The agreement also says:

"There will be safeguards to ensure that all sections of the community can participate and work together successfully in the operation of these [devolved] institutions and that all sections of the community are protected, including..... arrangements to provide that key decisions and legislation are proofed to ensure that they do not infringe the ECHR and any Bill of Rights for Northern Ireland".

"The Assembly may appoint a special Committee to examine and report on whether a measure or proposal for legislation is in conformity with equality requirements, including the ECHR/Bill of Rights."

"The Assembly will have authority to pass primary legislation for Northern Ireland in devolved areas, subject to: (a) the ECHR and any Bill of Rights for Northern Ireland supplementing it which, if the courts found to be breached, would render the relevant legislation null and void".

It is clear from these references that the signatories supported the creation of a Bill of Rights for Northern Ireland and expected one to be enacted. However, there is no Bill of Rights for Northern Ireland.

A substantial consultation document on a Bill of Rights for Northern Ireland was published in September 2001 by the Northern Ireland Human Rights Commission, but did not lead to legislation.

While the St Andrews Agreement amended various aspects of how government operated in Northern Ireland, it did not attempt to remove the apparent commitment to a Bill of Rights. Indeed, it contained a promise to act in furtherance of the Bill of Rights.

The St Andrews Agreement says:

"The Government will continue to actively promote the advancement of human rights, equality and mutual respect.

In the pursuit of which we commit to the following: .... We will establish a forum on a Bill of Rights and convene its inaugural meeting in December 2006."

The Northern Ireland Human Rights Commission's Forum produced recommendations in December 2008, but the Forum itself was boycotted by both the DUP and the Catholic Church. Both rejected the outcome because of their position opposing abortion, which was not accepted by the Forum.

The Forum recommended that a Bill of Rights for Northern Ireland should include rights supplementary to the ECHR, including socio-economic rights, children's rights and environmental rights, as well as broadening the definition of a 'victim'. The Northern Ireland Office rejected the majority of the NIHRC's recommendations on the basis that the rights were not specific to the circumstances of Northern Ireland as required by the terms of reference and that they might be more appropriately addressed as part of the debate over a UK Bill of Rights.

The Northern Ireland Human Rights Commission continues to support the adoption and implementation of a Bill of Rights for Northern Ireland.

A model draft Bill of Rights for Northern Ireland has been produced by the Transitional Justice Institution, an Ulster University research institute. The draft Bill of Rights is published at:

https://www.ulster.ac.uk/__data/assets/pdf_file/0017/205451/Bill-of-Rights-NI-Draft-Model-Bill-June-2017.pdf

14

MAKING UNIONISTS COMFORTABLE IN A NEW IRELAND

By *Pat McArt*

There are just over 883,000 people who classify themselves as Protestant in the 2011 Census; 48% of the population of Northern Ireland. A majority of these would regard themselves as both unionist and British – and would probably continue to do so after reunification.

Many Protestants are comfortable at present living in the Republic, especially as the Catholic influence over the state has declined. Andy Pollak, a respected commentator and former Irish Times religious affairs correspondent, spent a long time working in Belfast. "I believe in 2015 the Republic of Ireland is a good place for Protestants," he suggested. "In the words of former Labour Party leader, Ruairi Quinn, Ireland is now a post-Catholic pluralist republic."

Pollak went on to say that Garret FitzGerald's view that Irish society had changed more rapidly than any other society in Western Europe in recent times held true – nearly 10% of the population is now foreign born."The Church of Ireland and other Protestant churches are growing again helped both by immigrants and by Catholics often disillusioned by a lack of spiritual and moral leadership (most scandalously by child abusing priests) in the majority church."

Pollak added: "Irish Catholicism is itself becoming more Protestant with far more emphasis on liberty of the individual conscience and participation by grass roots members than in the previously authoritarian institutional church. None of this is any kind of attempt to persuade northern Protestants and unionists to give up their Britishness. However, they should realise the Republic isn't such an alien place these days – in many way it is more open-minded, tolerant and liberal society than the north: and secondly, it wouldn't do them any harm to admit they too have a little bit of Irishness in their make-up and it might be interesting to visit the south to explore that."

Today many members of the Protestant churches are centre stage in Irish life. Bono of U2 bestrides the music world like no other. Ireland's most loved sportswoman is Katie Taylor. Judge Susan Denham is a former president of the High Court. Ivan Yates is one of the country's favourite broadcasters, while Graham Norton is beloved just about everywhere. Until recently there were two Protestant cabinet ministers, Heather Humphreys and Jan O'Sullivan, while one of the most colourful politicians in the Oireachtas is David Norris, who has been joined in the Irish senate by former Ulster Farmer's Union president Ian Marshall.

Catherine McGuinness, retired Supreme Court Judge, argued at the Merriman Summer School that Irish Protestants can be, and were, as Irish as anyone else.

Former Irish Attorney General, John Rodgers, in an article in 1998, suggested that the current Irish constitution should be amended to recognise what he describes as 'the plural origins' of our people and the absence of an acknowledged history and common allegiance. The preamble, he argued, should include the phrase that 'the republic is established for all members of the community on a basis of equality and respect.'

The New Ireland Forum, established by Garret FitzGerald in 1983, recommended that references to God be toned down and that references to Christian God be removed. In line with this and the Citizens Rights Charter suggestion, which appeared to be advocated by civic unionists, the religious formula for oaths of office would be removed and judges would make a secular declaration rather than religious.

There is a need to have a more broad based Irish identity, which includes a British identity. Ulster Unionist politician, Christopher McGimpsey, didn't underestimate the difficulties involved when he described the formation of such a definition as "being as simple as nailing jelly to a wall", but it needs to be done.

A number of steps could be considered to assist those who identify as unionists and British to feel comfortable within the new Ireland, and to offer their loyalty and commitment to the new state.

These might include:

1   A Bill of Rights respecting the British identity on this island including the valued place the unionist community has for the Royal family;

2   Ireland to rejoin the Commonwealth. Strengthening where possible and practicable, the 'East-West' relationship would give considerable comfort to people who see Scotland or England as the motherland.

3   Respect for the marching traditions of both cultures, particularly in regard to Orange parades, but subject to an overriding consent by hosting communities;

4   The right for those born in Ireland to opt for either Irish or British nationality and identity, with equality for all those holding British passports;

5   Guaranteed security of tenure of land for all - no redistribution of land;

6   Debate on possible devolution – retention of Stormont for either the six or nine counties, as well as other provincial or federal government arrangements;

7   Military forces for each administrative area north and south to be drawn from each respective area;

8   Parity of esteem for all languages by way of legislation - English, Irish, Ulster Scots.

9   Reaffirmation of Ireland as a secular state, with equal

recognition of Catholic, Protestant and other religions guaranteed and respect for their identities and independence;

10 New flags, anthem and other regional and national symbols to be discussed, with the objective of achieving consensus prior to any vote on reunification. Elements of the Union Flag ('Union Jack') might be incorporated in a new flag or flags, or the Union Flag be flown on designated days on main government buildings alongside the tricolour or new national flag on national public holidays, including the 12th July and the UK Sovereign's birthday.

11 Make the 12th July a bank holiday in the Republic as recommended by the ICTU.

12 Ensure that judges in the new republic are trained in the laws of Scotland as they are now in English law, to recognise the value unionists have in their Scots–Ulster links.

13 Irish citizens are precluded from being members of the Privy Council or holding a knighthood. This disbarment should be ended.

14 Restriction on religious ministers standing for election needs to be reviewed.

15 British citizens within a united island would be able to vote, subject to residency requirements, as is the UK situation for Irish citizens.

16 There should be legal and constitutional protection against discrimination for people who do not speak Irish.

17 Requirements for compulsory Irish from students, lawyers, etc, should be removed.

18 The International Court of Justice should be recognised, acting as a safeguard for unionists to ensure rights are interpreted, implemented and protected.

19   In the event of a six or nine county Stormont
      administration being restored under a unified island, an
      ombudsman should be appointed to ensure that
      ministers carry out their functions in compliance with
      the oath they take to obtain office under the Good
      Friday Agreement.

Des Murphy SC has recommended that an international mediator should produce a set of proposals for consideration, as was done prior to the peace process. This would be considered within the framework of the Good Friday Agreement.

Professor Brice Dickson, a law lecturer at Queen's University, explained to the New Ireland Forum that rights conferred under Articles 40 to 44 may be uncomfortable to some from the unionist tradition. They may be unhappy to express loyalty to the Irish President in place of their loyalty to the Crown. In developing an all-island constitution or Bill of Rights these sensitivities need to be considered in language and tone and content.

(Articles 40 to 44 of the Irish Constitution are reproduced in full as Appendix One.)

15
WHAT NOW?

For the first time since partition, reunification of Ireland has become a realistic possibility. The twin pressures of Brexit and demography have changed the political context. To add to this, the failure of devolved government to create a financially sustainable Northern Ireland is encouraging people to consider different arrangements for future governance.

It is essential to recognise, though, that whatever governance structure is adopted for Northern Ireland, and whatever jurisdiction it is part of, the same underlying problems must be addressed. Northern Ireland is not self-financing, it is wasteful and it needs fundamental reform.

Those who argue for a united Ireland need to recognise these facts, otherwise they are engaged in a level of dishonesty that is similar to those Brexiteers who pretended that leaving the EU would be simple to negotiate on terms that were beneficial for the UK. The challenges of a united Ireland are severe. At their heart is addressing the economic weaknesses that are inherent in Northern Ireland.

There are around 50,000 more people in the public sector workforce in Northern Ireland than there would be if it were the same size, pro rata, as that of the Republic of Ireland or England. This follows a process of constriction that has already cut by 20,000 the number of people employed in the public sector in Northern Ireland. No trade unionist can comfortably argue for the loss of jobs. Equally, though, inefficient public services are a tax burden on the wider population, including those on low incomes. Gradual reform leading to more efficient public services, with support for those who leave to move to other jobs, is a legitimate objective.

It needs to be recognised that not only would around 50,000 job losses be devastating, if mishandled, for those involved, but it could also worsen Northern Ireland's economic problems. If those 50,000 people lost income it would increase welfare benefit costs, reduce tax revenues and reduce spending on retail and other private sector activities. While in England the reduction in public sector jobs has been more than balanced by private sector job creation, many of those new jobs are undertaken by people who are self-employed, outside minimum wage protection and in casualised employment. An effective strategy is required to shift, over time, a large number of reasonably well paid and protected public sector workers into good jobs in the private sector.

Reform is needed urgently with regard to Northern Ireland's health service. Waiting lists and waiting times are too long. It has been argued that the NHS in Northern Ireland requires more funding, which is true. It is also said that some of the NHS funds are wasted in inefficient PFI contracts, which is also true. But the Bengoa and Compton reports have made clear that root and branch reform cannot be avoided. In essence, we need fewer acute hospitals, improved specialised service provision, expanded primary care, more training of doctors and greater focus on ill-health prevention. Getting on with those reforms is an urgent priority – it should either be agreed by all parties prior to the resuscitation of the Northern Ireland Executive and Assembly, or else the UK government needs to act directly with regard to this specific challenge.

For many, many people in Northern Ireland, reassurance that they would continue to receive healthcare free at the point of delivery is their major issue regarding Irish reunification. Politically, a united Ireland is perhaps unachievable until a free at point of delivery, all-island, high quality, healthcare system is provided. A ten year timeframe for political unification, alongside the creation of that healthcare system, seems a reasonable objective.

It is probably unrealistic for Northern Ireland's parties to act as if the UK government, and British taxpayers, will indefinitely accept a large subvention to Northern Ireland. Whatever the figure, the subvention is large. While local authorities in England are dealing with the loss of most of their funding, there has been a much lower level of austerity applied in Northern Ireland. Policy-makers in the north of Ireland need to act with greater focus and urgency in redesigning services to reduce their cost. Specifically, the sectarianisation of public services needs to be, as far as possible, ended. According to the Alliance Party, the lack of integrated public service delivery costs perhaps £1bn a year – pure waste, which supports and promotes continued social division.

At the heart of Northern Ireland's economic problems is unbalanced public spending. Public finances need to be reprioritised, with much more allocated towards skills and infrastructure, while addressing regional economic imbalances. Productivity in Northern Ireland is horribly weak, which points to a lack of investment, insufficient skills and inadequate infrastructure. Addressing this requires the expansion of the north's universities, improvements in the vocational skills provision and as far as possible ensuring every person in the labour market has the skills that can provide them with worthwhile, valued and well paid employment.

This should be backed by a transport system that enables people to travel around Northern Ireland quickly and enables businesses to get goods to market quickly and efficiently. There needs to be a digital infrastructure that gives people even in remote rural areas access to high speed broadband and a strong mobile signal. Without these improvements, our productivity will not improve and inward (and indigenous) investment will not arrive in sufficient quantities.

Failing to deal with these challenges will not assist with either of the competing tasks – of arguing for a united Ireland, or retention within the United Kingdom. Reform has to be tackled under either scenario. While the Good Friday Agreement produced an unsettled peace, it failed to deliver economic prosperity. It did not provide the sea change in employment that is arguably a prerequisite for a more settled peace, which creates prosperity for all.

Denial of the need for radical reform under any governance arrangement damages the credibility of those seeking other changes, including Irish reunification. There is a strong argument for saying that the lack of greater and faster economic expansion following the Good Friday Agreement is not only responsible for stubbornly high levels of unemployment – in particular among young working class men – but also the low levels of economic optimism and aspirations across much of Northern Ireland society. That, in turn, feeds into continued support by some for organised criminality and paramilitarism.

Similarly, the sectarian divisions within our society will not disappear simply because republicans/nationalists are no longer in a minority, but unionists are. A settled peace requires different communities to be at ease with each other. Failing to address this risks a negative reaction by the southern electorate against Irish reunification in a border poll. The prospect of southern voters saying 'no' while northern voters perhaps opt 'yes' should be of greater concern than it has been.

There is something peculiar, as well as misleading, about the current and ongoing debate about the crisis in Northern Ireland. It has a touch of the 'Emperor's new clothes', or the 'elephant in the room', about it. While the contemporary political arguments focus on the demands for an Irish Language Act, an Ulster Scots Language Act, addressing legacy issues, same sex marriage, women's reproductive rights and allocating blame for RHI – and all these issues are important and deserve being resolved - the bigger and more challenging debate that is largely avoided is how we restructure our society. This is not just about removing the sectarian divisions, but also how we substantially reform our public finances in ways that lead to the creation of a vibrant economy that offers opportunities for all within Northern Ireland. There needs to be greater consideration of the reality that Northern Ireland – along with much of England – is one of the poorest regions of northern Europe and that there needs to be fundamental policy change in order to turn this around.

There is a need for mature conversations, today. Those discussions need to consider more the values that are shared, less on the things that divide. As Peter Sheridan remarked (in section four), the rights that are of most value are those demanded by one community on behalf of another. So republicans need to be arguing the case for people (now, and in the future) who identify as British but live in Ireland to be entitled to a British passport. If the right is provided under the Good Friday Agreement to those who were born in Northern Ireland to identify as Irish, then why not similarly to those born in the south and who identify as British?

It is important for the UK government to revert to a position of neutrality on the future of Northern Ireland's constitutional status. That position has been dangerously abandoned by Theresa May because of her need to rely on DUP votes, and before her by David Cameron's desire to have UUP MPs in the House of Commons take the Conservative whip. Both prime ministers have played party politics with the Irish peace process.

The UK government must again commit to being neutral on Northern Ireland's status. Indeed, it should go further by promising to support the interests and wellbeing of people who identify as British even if Northern Ireland as a whole decides to be part of a united Ireland. This is likely to require some continued, tapered, financial support to assist a united Ireland to succeed. Both nations gain from the success and strength of the other.

Germany is widely regarded – including in Karl Huebner's report – as being an example of how national reunification can produce success and a gain for all. However, this is a simplistic analysis of the German situation. East Germany continues to lag in terms of wealth, employment and productivity behind West Germany. True, it has made major strides in catching up. But many people in East Germany expected faster progress. And many in the West are resentful of the financial cost of absorbing East Germany. The results of reunification have included economic expansion, but also anger at the sense that the east was 'absorbed' and a rise, especially in the east, of the far right Alternative for Deutschland party (AfD). Lessons from Germany include not making excessive claims for what can be achieved and also ensuring that the incoming communities feel welcomed and valued.

The complexity of the arguments for, and against, Irish reunification means that the discussion needs to be mature and honest. The integration of the north into a united Ireland should not be attempted as if the north is a critically ill patient going into intensive care. The Brexit referendum – full of misrepresentations and false hopes – provides a blueprint for how to not do things. A rushed border poll could lead to a result that is similarly not respected by the losing side. Proper democracy involves the telling of truth and the challenging interrogation of claims and counter-claims. It requires time.

Although Brexit provides the context for discussion of a united Ireland, it would be unwise, and unfair, for any referendum on it to take place until we can be confident on its effect on Northern Ireland, Great Britain and the Republic of Ireland. While it seems likely that Northern Ireland will be damaged by Brexit, it is possible that the Republic will also be damaged – and perhaps to the extent that it would be reluctant to simultaneously deal with the challenge of integrating the north into its jurisdiction. One of the lessons of Brexit is that governments sometimes do not have the capacity to deal with more than one major political challenge at a time.

While the creation of a united Ireland is now possible, the debate must be handled with care and mutual respect. If the case for a united Ireland perceived by unionists and loyalists to be put forward solely by Sinn Fein, or led by them, it will be rejected by many. Similarly, if the case for continued membership of the United Kingdom is led by the TUV and hardened loyalists, it will not be listened to by many nationalists.

There need to be sensible conversations with open minded unionists about the role of unionists and loyalists in a united Ireland (should it happen) and how that new society can demonstrate that it values the engagement of unionists and loyalists. Interviews published in this study demonstrate that there are political leaders of unionism who are willing to have those conversations – not because they want a united Ireland, but because they recognise its creation is possible (and probable over the longer term) and they want to protect the interests of the people they represent. This is sensible realpolitik. There is no reason why more of those conversations should not take place immediately, led in particular by the universities of Northern Ireland and the Republic.

These discussions should also involve figures from the United States and Europe, recognising the value of past contributions in healing divisions and bringing different sides together. It is likely that a successful reunification project will need practical and also financial support from outside, which these discussions could assist.

Northern Ireland needs to plan for the future – and those plans are very similar whether it is to remain as part of the UK, or become part of a united Ireland. It needs to increase tax income, reduce public spending on day to day items while increasing investment for the long term, increase the size of the economy, reform its public sector and create many more jobs. The UK government should be closely involved in all these areas, recognising that the promised 'peace dividend' did not flow from the Good Friday Agreement.

Meanwhile, the Irish government needs to continue its existing programme of reform – especially if it is serious about seeking Irish reunification. While growing numbers of people in the north are jealous of the strength of the economy in the south, large numbers will reject reunification without an NHS being created in the Republic. The health service is a frequently cited concern by people in the north when the concept of a united Ireland is discussed – and is probably the major challenge to be overcome. SláinteCare represents the opportunity to improve healthcare in the Republic, reduce health inequalities and provide a more cost-efficient health system. It also represents probably the most important initiative that could enable Irish reunification. Faster progress is therefore required towards full implementation of SláinteCare.

Other concerns are also cited by people in the north when considering reunification. One of these is the failure of housing policy in the Republic. (Housing policy in the north can also be regarded as a failure – just less badly so.) Regional policy is also needs to be strengthened in the Republic, especially with regard to border areas such as Donegal. (The north's sub-regional policy is significantly worse, especially with regard to border areas such as Derry.)

Cultural issues must be addressed. Philip Gilliland (in section 4) suggested the Irish state needs to go much further in vocalisation its recognition of the role of Protestants in the Republic. This is a role that should perhaps be led by the President. And the Irish state could embrace the global role of Irish Presbyterians, including in the foundation of the United States and in their roles as leaders of the US and Commonwealth nations.

Ireland's national broadcaster, RTE, needs to be more inclusive with regards to Northern Ireland if the island is to feel more cohesive (as Jane Morrice explains in section 4). That involves RTE explaining to people in the south more of what is happening in the north, but also being more easily available to television viewers across the north. The membership of more northern Protestants in the Senate would be another welcome step.

Irish reunification is only possible if a majority in both jurisdictions want it. But it also requires changes to how those jurisdictions operate – and in the case of the Republic, some of those changes need to begin now and be rolled-out quickly. Changes that demonstrate that Ireland as a whole values the traditions, cultures and contributions of people from Protestant, unionist and loyalist backgrounds are essential.

Northern Ireland must also change. A report from John FitzGerald[179] argues that were the Irish state to take over the subvention that Northern Ireland receives from the UK government, this could make citizens in the south permanently poorer by 15%. The misleading media coverage of that argument rests on two flawed assumptions. Firstly, the level of subvention potentially transferring to a reunified state would not actually be in the region of €11bn: it is clear (see section twelve) that the real subvention is around half of that. Secondly, the report assumes that Northern Ireland is unable to address that remaining subvention – and that a reunified state is unable to reduce it. Those seeking a united Ireland must therefore do all they can to cut the subvention if they are to successfully make the case for Irish reunification.

A ten year period provides a reasonable transition period in which to make major inroads into Northern Ireland's subvention requirement. It should also provide sufficient time to establish SláinteCare in the

Republic – in line with the Oireachtas committee's recommended implementation period. Only after these concerns have been fully addressed can there be confidence that referendums in both the north and the south would be likely to succeed.

But creating greater cohesion between all communities across the island is an even greater priority, and also will take time. Simply achieving a united Ireland is not enough. It has to be an integrated nation, a new society, which brings people together and increases collective prosperity and wellbeing.

Attempting to achieve a massively difficult task too quickly is a path to confusion and failure. Irish reunification – just like German reunification – must be a long term project if it is to be successful. A ten year plan to achieve it provides that strong foundation that can and should lead to success.

APPENDIX ONE:

THE ROLE OF THE GOOD FRIDAY AGREEMENT

By Mr Justice Richard Humphreys

The following article, originally published in the main by the Irish Examiner, with an additional section published by the Irish News, is republished by permission of Richard Humphreys.

The Good Friday Agreement, signed 20 years ago, was meant to mark a new start to relationships within these islands. But the promise of the agreement is under challenge as never before.

At least five significant areas of uncertainty may lie ahead. The most immediate uncertainty is Brexit and the challenges it may pose for relationships on the island and for the invisible border. After Brexit, there are fears that there may be attempts in Britain to repeal the Human Rights Act.

In Northern Ireland, Stormont remains gridlocked, the key Good Friday institutions are not functioning and the rights and equality commitments have not been fully implemented. Even if devolution is restored, there are no guarantees to prevent a future collapse. And at the end of the process lies the debate on the ultimate constitutional uncertainty as to the final status of Northern Ireland, either in a united Ireland or a United Kingdom.

The decision by a majority of the UK electorate to leave the EU — outvoting the local majorities to remain in Northern Ireland, Scotland, Gibraltar, and Greater London — threatens many of the intangible benefits of the agreement.

The Good Friday Agreement is about co-existence, building bridges, overcoming differences, softening borders. Brexit, whatever it achieves for the UK, does little for Ireland and certainly runs the risk of deepening divisions on the island.

For the DUP that was perhaps one of the attractions — putting blue water between themselves and the mistrusted republic. But that approach runs the risk of backfiring — Brexit has significantly changed the debate on Irish unity.

That issue is no longer a black and white clash of identities, UK vs Ireland. It is now about whether the people of Northern Ireland want to be part of what is seen as an inward-looking UK or an outward-looking EU, with all of the rights that go with that.

Whether Irish unity is a good thing or a bad thing can be left to political debate. But Brexit has transformed the terms of the discussion.

In the short term, all sides are agreed as to the need to avoid a hard border. How this will be achieved is still being discussed but strong regulatory alignment, at least within the island of Ireland if not between Ireland and the UK, seems likely to be a key element of the ultimate agreement.

Once Brexit has taken effect, from March 2019, there are concerns that the political forces that delivered British withdrawal from the EU will move on to a new agenda to endeavour to repeal the Human Rights Act. That would be a clear breach of the Good Friday Agreement. The agreement commits Britain to incorporating the European Convention on Human Rights into UK law.

Replacing it unilaterally with a purely British bill of rights, with no link to European law, would violate one of the central rights commitments of the 1998 agreement.

Making the European convention part of the law has been a huge change in mindset with the UK, and to a lesser extent in Ireland. It means that the debate on whether laws and actions comply with European human rights law can be discussed in domestic courts, rather than just in Strasbourg. It would be a major step backwards for the protection of human rights if that link were to be broken.

In Northern Ireland, meanwhile, the gridlock in Stormont continues. Here, there is an imperative need to return to the wording of the agreement and ensure its full implementation.

On the one hand, the unique power-sharing arrangements envisaged by the agreement mean that political parties must operate it in good faith. It is a breach of the agreement for them to pull out of government merely due to political disagreements.

On the other hand, the agreement also commits all participants to upholding equality of rights between the two traditions. That is set out in the strongest possible language in the agreement. That inevitably means that some form of legal protection for the Irish language will have to be enacted.

It is totally unsustainable to have the commitments to parity of esteem side by side with minimal status for Irish — for example, take the statutory prohibition that exists at present banning any language other than English from being used in Northern Irish courts.

The commitment to parity of esteem also poses significant questions for both Ireland and the UK more broadly. To what extent is Ireland recognising the British identity? Would there be merit in reconsidering the concept of allowing British citizens to vote in referenda, as proposed in the 1980s?

Would membership of the Commonwealth be worth considering, seeing as it has now changed so completely and become so much less threatening to republican identities since Ireland left it in 1949?

And on the British side, much antiquated anti-Catholic legislation remains on the statute book. This sends an unhealthy, even destructive message to those in Northern Ireland who trade on superiority and discrimination.

Going beyond the current impasse, there will come a point when the structural weaknesses of the agreement will have to be looked at. The agreement has two clear weaknesses. First of all, it makes it far too easy for a minority to block legislation.

If Stormont was allowed to legislate on a simple majority basis (like the Dail does), a huge range of issues such as the Irish language, LGBT rights, and other matters would simply be taken off the table.

Rights-based legislation would simply be passed. Instead, a blocking mechanism which was intended to protect rights has become a means of preventing the enactment of rights. That is a recipe for gridlock and stalemate into the indefinite future.

The second, even more serious, weakness of the agreement is that it is all-too-easy for one of the major parties to simply pull down the institutions at any time and prevent them from re-starting. In such a situation, all parties other than the major ones are rendered irrelevant.

Again, what started as a protection for minorities and rights has become a mechanism for stagnation. There is no good alternative to devolution — the alternative is simply British rule with Irish advisory input, assuming the British side wants to hear that advice. On recent evidence that is not entirely obvious.

Nobody has yet come up with a better alternative to the agreement so it is certainly not time for it to be scrapped or anything like it. But at some stage there must be an opportunity to review and improve it in order to anticipate and head off problems into the future.

Finally, at the end of the road of constitutional debate lies the ultimate question — should Northern Ireland remain as is or become part of a united Ireland? While I would stand on the neutral sidelines on that issue, it is important — indeed essential — that the debate on possible unity takes place within the terms envisaged by the agreement. Two points are noteworthy: When is unity appropriate, and what sort of unity are we talking about?

As to when unity might happen, the agreement is clear — the mechanisms for unity are the clearest parts of the agreement. A border poll happens when the UK Northern secretary so decides — and she must call one when she thinks it will pass.

The decision of a simple majority of those present and validly voting is decisive — 50% plus one, subject to a similar vote in the South. There is no requirement for a super-majority. There is no requirement for unionist consent or parallel consent.

Contrary to some loyalist proposals, raising the threshold for unity – for example, to a super-majority – is ruled out. That does not mean that 50% plus one for unity would be a great situation. Obviously if there is change, the more broadly based the support the better. But legally, a simple majority is sufficient, because a simple majority to stay in the UK would also be sufficient.

Unionism is not a superior position to nationalism, so the test must be reciprocal. For the same reason, there is no principle of unionist consent to a united Ireland, because there is no principle requiring nationalist consent to a United Kingdom. That does not mean unionist sentiment can be ignored - far from it. The agreement commits to all sides to recognising equality of rights for both traditions.

The requirement of a simple majority is not a sectarian headcount or crude tribal majoritarianism because it is a reciprocal tie-breaker for the ultimate constitutional issue, which is balanced by counter-majoritarian protections on other issues.

But as to what sort of unity are we talking about, the agreement rules out the old-style, four green fields nationalism. It requires recognition of the British identity into the future, including an ongoing right to British citizenship for the people of Northern Ireland.

And above all the agreement has no termination clause. So it remains in force even if unity is achieved. That means a power-sharing executive and assembly indefinitely into the future.

If there ever was a majority for unity, life would continue as normal in Stormont. MPs would go to Dublin as TDs rather than to Westminster, but Dublin's role in legislating for the North would be quite limited, much as Westminster's is now.

Whether Brexit, unity, or any other changes are a good or a bad idea can be left to political debate. But in all the change and uncertainty, the agreement must be explained and upheld.

The key to negotiating the huge challenges ahead is to keep the agreement's terms firmly in mind — the protection of rights for all, equality between the traditions, and strong protective institutions that can weather constitutional change.

If Northern Ireland as a functioning entity can be allowed to bed down, if rights can be afforded to all, and if the agreement is upheld and implemented, maybe the stale deadlock of the clash of constitutional identities may not matter so much in the end.

Richard Humphreys is a judge of the High Court in Dublin. His latest book, Beyond the Border: The Good Friday Agreement and Irish Unity after Brexit is out now from Merrion Press.

APPENDIX TWO:

ARTICLES 40 TO 44
OF THE IRISH CONSTITUTION

FUNDAMENTAL RIGHTS

PERSONAL RIGHTS
ARTICLE 40

1   All citizens shall, as human persons, be held equal
       before the law.

       This shall not be held to mean that the State shall not
       in its enactments have due regard to differences of
       capacity, physical and moral, and of social function.

2 1°   Titles of nobility shall not be conferred by the State.

2°   No title of nobility or of honour may be accepted by
       any citizen except with the prior approval of the
       Government.

3 1°   The State guarantees in its laws to respect, and, as far
       as practicable, by its laws to defend and vindicate the
       personal rights of the citizen.

2°   The State shall, in particular, by its laws protect as best
       it may from unjust attack and, in the case of injustice
       done, vindicate the life, person, good name, and
       property rights of every citizen.

3°   The State acknowledges the right to life of the unborn and, with due regard to the equal right to life of the mother, guarantees in its laws to respect, and, as far as practicable, by its laws to defend and vindicate that right.

This subsection shall not limit freedom to travel between the State and another state.

This subsection shall not limit freedom to obtain or make available, in the State, subject to such conditions as may be laid down by law, information relating to services lawfully available in another state.

4 1°   No citizen shall be deprived of his personal liberty save in accordance with law.

2°   Upon complaint being made by or on behalf of any person to the High Court or any judge thereof alleging that such person is being unlawfully detained, the High Court and any and every judge thereof to whom such complaint is made shall forthwith enquire into the said complaint and may order the person in whose custody such person is detained to produce the body of such person before the High Court on a named day and to certify in writing the grounds of his detention, and the High Court shall, upon the body of such person being produced before that Court and after giving the person in whose custody he is detained an opportunity of justifying the detention, order the release of such person from such detention unless satisfied that he is being detained in accordance with the law.

3°   Where the body of a person alleged to be unlawfully

detained is produced before the High Court in pursuance of an order in that behalf made under this section and that Court is satisfied that such person is being detained in accordance with a law but that such law is invalid having regard to the provisions of this Constitution, the High Court shall refer the question of the validity of such law to the Court of Appeal by way of case stated and may, at the time of such reference or at any time thereafter, allow the said person to be at liberty on such bail and subject to such conditions as the High Court shall fix until the Court of Appeal has determined the question so referred to it.

4°   The High Court before which the body of a person alleged to be unlawfully detained is to be produced in pursuance of an order in that behalf made under this section shall, if the President of the High Court or, if he is not available, the senior judge of that Court who is available so directs in respect of any particular case, consist of three judges and shall, in every other case, consist of one judge only.

5°   Nothing in this section, however, shall be invoked to prohibit, control, or interfere with any act of the Defence Forces during the existence of a state of war or armed rebellion.

6°   Provision may be made by law for the refusal of bail by a court to a person charged with a serious offence where it is reasonably considered necessary to prevent the commission of a serious offence by that person.

5   The dwelling of every citizen is inviolable and shall not be forcibly entered save in accordance with law.

6 1°   The State guarantees liberty for the exercise of the following rights, subject to public order and morality: –

i   The right of the citizens to express freely their convictions and opinions.

The education of public opinion being, however, a matter of such grave import to the common good, the State shall endeavour to ensure that organs of public opinion, such as the radio, the press, the cinema, while preserving their rightful liberty of expression, including criticism of Government policy, shall not be used to undermine public order or morality or the authority of the State.

The publication or utterance of blasphemous, seditious, or indecent matter is an offence which shall be punishable in accordance with law.

ii   The right of the citizens to assemble peaceably and without arms.

Provision may be made by law to prevent or control meetings which are determined in accordance with law to be calculated to cause a breach of the peace or to be a danger or nuisance to the general public and to prevent or control meetings in the vicinity of either House of the Oireachtas.

iii   The right of the citizens to form associations and unions.
Laws, however, may be enacted for the regulation

and control in the public interest of the exercise of the foregoing right.

2°   Laws regulating the manner in which the right of forming associations and unions and the right of free assembly may be exercised shall contain no political, religious or class discrimination.

THE FAMILY
ARTICLE 41

1 1°   The State recognises the Family as the natural primary and fundamental unit group of Society, and as a moral institution possessing inalienable and imprescriptible rights, antecedent and superior to all positive law.

2°   The State, therefore, guarantees to protect the Family in its constitution and authority, as the necessary basis of social order and as indispensable to the welfare of the Nation and the State.

2 1°   In particular, the State recognises that by her life within the home, woman gives to the State a support without which the common good cannot be achieved.

2°   The State shall, therefore, endeavour to ensure that mothers shall not be obliged by economic necessity to engage in labour to the neglect of their duties in the home.

3 1°   The State pledges itself to guard with special care the institution of Marriage, on which the Family is founded, and to protect it against attack.

2°   A Court designated by law may grant a dissolution of marriage where, but only where, it is satisfied that –

i   at the date of the institution of the proceedings, the spouses have lived apart from one another for a period of, or periods amounting to, at least four years during the previous five years,

ii   there is no reasonable prospect of a reconciliation between the spouses,

iii   such provision as the Court considers proper having regard to the circumstances exists or will be made for the spouses, any children of either or both of them and any other person prescribed by law, and

iv   any further conditions prescribed by law are complied with.

3°   No person whose marriage has been dissolved under the civil law of any other State but is a subsisting valid marriage under the law for the time being in force within the jurisdiction of the Government and Parliament established by this Constitution shall be capable of contracting a valid marriage within that jurisdiction during the lifetime of the other party to the marriage so dissolved.

4   Marriage may be contracted in accordance with law by two persons without distinction as to their sex.

EDUCATION
ARTICLE 42

1   The State acknowledges that the primary and natural educator of the child is the Family and guarantees to respect the inalienable right and duty of parents to provide, according to their means, for the religious and moral, intellectual, physical and social education of their children.

2   Parents shall be free to provide this education in their homes or in private schools or in schools recognised or established by the State.

3 1°   The State shall not oblige parents in violation of their conscience and lawful preference to send their children to schools established by the State, or to any particular type of school designated by the State.

2°   The State shall, however, as guardian of the common good, require in view of actual conditions that the children receive a certain minimum education, moral, intellectual and social.

4   The State shall provide for free primary education and shall endeavour to supplement and give reasonable aid to private and corporate educational initiative, and, when the public good requires it, provide other educational facilities or institutions with due regard, however, for the rights of parents, especially in the matter of religious and moral formation.

CHILDREN
ARTICLE 42A

1   The State recognises and affirms the natural and imprescriptible rights of all children and shall, as far as practicable, by its laws protect and vindicate those rights.

2 1°   In exceptional cases, where the parents, regardless of their marital status, fail in their duty towards their children to such extent that the safety or welfare of any of their children is likely to be prejudicially affected, the State as guardian of the common good shall, by proportionate means as provided by law, endeavour to supply the place of the parents, but always with due regard for the natural and imprescriptible rights of the child.

2°   Provision shall be made by law for the adoption of any child where the parents have failed for such a period of time as may be prescribed by law in their duty towards the child and where the best interests of the child so require.

3   Provision shall be made by law for the voluntary placement for adoption and the adoption of any child.

4 1°   Provision shall be made by law that in the resolution of all proceedings—

    i   brought by the State, as guardian of the common good, for the purpose of preventing the safety and welfare of any child from being prejudicially affected, or

   ii   concerning the adoption, guardianship or custody
of, or access to, any child,
the best interests of the child shall be the
paramount consideration.

2°   Provision shall be made by law for securing, as far as
practicable, that in all proceedings referred to in
subsection 1° of this section in respect of any child
who is capable of forming his or her own views, the
views of the child shall be ascertained and given due
weight having regard to the age and maturity of the
child.

PRIVATE PROPERTY
ARTICLE 43

1 1°   The State acknowledges that man, in virtue of his
rational being, has the natural right, antecedent to
positive law, to the private ownership of external
goods.

2°   The State accordingly guarantees to pass no law
attempting to abolish the right of private ownership or
the general right to transfer, bequeath, and inherit
property.

2 1°   The State recognises, however, that the exercise of the
rights mentioned in the foregoing provisions of this

Article ought, in civil society, to be regulated by the principles of social justice.

2°   The State, accordingly, may as occasion requires delimit by law the exercise of the said rights with a view to reconciling their exercise with the exigencies of the common good.

RELIGION
ARTICLE 44

1   The State acknowledges that the homage of public worship is due to Almighty God. It shall hold His Name in reverence, and shall respect and honour religion.

2 1°   Freedom of conscience and the free profession and practice of religion are, subject to public order and morality, guaranteed to every citizen.

2°   The State guarantees not to endow any religion.

3°   The State shall not impose any disabilities or make any discrimination on the ground of religious profession, belief or status.

4°   Legislation providing State aid for schools shall not discriminate between schools under the management of different religious denominations, nor be such as to affect prejudicially the right of any child to attend a school receiving public money without attending religious instruction at that school.

5°   Every religious denomination shall have the right to manage its own affairs, own, acquire and administer property, movable and immovable, and maintain institutions for religious or charitable purposes.

6°   The property of any religious denomination or any educational institution shall not be diverted save for necessary works of public utility and on payment of compensation.

APPENDIX THREE:

CRITICAL COMMENTS
from *Esmond Birnie*, Ulster University

Your paper proposes that the NI % public sector employment should be reduced to the RoI average rate implying 50,000 direct job losses. There could be long run benefit to NI economy if so-called "re-balancing" could be achieved- preferably through expansion of private sector rather than absolute decline of public.

BUT:

- If this reduction is done suddenly it becomes very problematic.
- Arguably, the Voluntary Exit Scheme was very much a second best (with perhaps unintended negative consequences- loss of some of the most experienced and best staff) but this would be VES on a super scale.
- How many of the 50,000 would get other jobs? What about multiplier effects?
- In fact 50,000 represents c 6% of total employment in NI. Once multiplier effects are included we start to get into the terrain of the upper scale losses (as in the Feb. 18 leak) produced by the Treasury modelling on Brexit. Your report describes such losses as "devastating".

THE FISCAL TRANSFER
Your paper suggests it is "only" the gap between identifiable spending and NI tax revenues which we should really worry about i.e. c. £5bn. rather than c. £10bn.

BUT:

- You need to assume about the "international services" (e.g. consul rep. for NI abroad and investment promotion) some of the following: (1.) RoI currently has great spare capacity and so could expand delivery without spending more or (2.) RoI could dramatically up the productivity of these services or (3.) the quantity/quality of services delivered per head post-unity would go down.

- You also need to assume no increase defence spending despite acquiring extra territory and coastline (and also assuming public order stays the same).

- Assuming the "rest of the UK" imposes no debt obligations on the new state (later on, you concede that dealing with NI's infrastructure may require borrowing).

- You've treated the accounting adjustment as just a technical (or paper) exercise but is it ? (amounting to £1bn p.a. re. capital consumption and proportionally larger in NI than UK average). But such Non-Market Capital Consumption is a reflection of higher proportional public sector capital stock- as this depreciates, to the extent it is replaced, there will be a "real" call on the NI+RoI taxpayers (a point you partly recognise when you call for GB to continue to pay for some infrastructure spend in NI).

- Interestingly, you impose on the generosity of the GB taxpayers by the possibility they may have to transition out of the transfer payment over a long period of time (and also pay for an infrastructure fund- which suggests to me the "real" transfer is more than £5bn p.a.).

HM TREASURY MODELLING

You quote the figures from the leaked document. It is very unsatisfactory that we have only the end figures without access to the underlying modelling (especially assumptions). It is probably reasonable to assume Treasury made similar assumptions to those made in their April 2016 document. So, we probably have the same flaws in their "gravity modelling" and their assumptions about very strong trade/output to productivity effects.

USE OF THE RECENT ROI NATIONAL ACCOUNTS
As the Dublin government and CSO Ireland have recognised, we cannot assume that in any meaningful sense RoI national output grew by 26% in 2015.

ROI COMPARATIVE WAGE LEVELS
It is not helpful to imply these are 50% higher than here in NI- cost of living differences.

(DEVOLVED) POLITICAL ECONOMY OF A UNITED IRELAND
Whatever the representational merits of devolution, I think there is a lot of evidence the Executive-UK government relationship has not worked well in terms of a sensible fiscal arrangement; Stormont has been "irresponsible" relying on HMG as the funder of last resort. Would that relationship be any better Stormont-Dublin, might it be even more problematic?

K. HUBNER'S MODELLING OF UNITY
I've critiqued this elsewhere (blog for ThisUnion website).

There is a general point- be it Brexit or German unification in 1990 or possibly Korean- about reservations about using these types of "Competitive General Equilibrium" models to make point predictions about the future and this even more so when economies undergo big structural changes.

Then specifically to this model re. NI and RoI (some of these points you make):

- The exchange rate situation is now very different.
- Their assumptions about the fiscal transfer seem very unclear.
- It is unrealistic to assume NI productivity would rapidly converge on the RoI level.
- There is no allowance for the negative impact of greater frictions to NI-GB trade (which is four times greater than NI-RoI).

IDENTITY ISSUES

As you say, people do value these. Sometimes more than economic gains/losses. I think it would be misunderstanding of the position of many pro-Union people to say they would settle for a status akin to, say, the Donegal Orangemen.

APPENDIX FOUR:

NON-ATTRIBUTABLE COMMENTS
from Senior Commentator

1)   **GDP AND PERFORMANCE:** Overreliance on GDP data to measure wealth or standards of living. The NI appearance at the top of happiness and quality of life charts should not be discounted, nor the employment / unemployment rate and other socio economic measures (homelessness, crime etc.) A young worker in Dublin trying to buy or rent a house compared to one in Belfast may not recognise the narrative in the report which paints NI as painfully far behind Ireland. Looking at many counties in Ireland it would be hard to draw that conclusion. And following on from that if Ireland has struggled to achieve growth in certain locations currently why would NI under Irish rule suddenly make better policy choices? Spending time in towns and cities in Ireland recently I would not suggest they would think they are 'streets ahead' of NI. Of course subsidy plays a (big) part in that but a wide range of indicators are worth referring to in showing the difference.

2)   **CONSENT:** Consent is mentioned but only in passing, the life and times survey matters I think and should perhaps get more coverage. If post Brexit the percentages wishing for change are not more compelling does this suggest that people simply don't understand how good it is in Ireland or could it be that point 1 is true and actually life in NI is actually rather good (lower personal tax, no prescription charges, subsidised education, no need for private health or schooling, low rates etc.)? If we credit the public with being able to know if they are happy or not it seems that those views need greater prominence. Watching Ireland's boom and bust partly as a result of the macro realities of being in Europe does suggest you are wanting to swap 'steady' performance for a much more volatile environment, that is not something everyone would choose I don't think.

3)   **SUBVENTION:** The subvention is complex (And Tom Healy's piece referred to in the annex is excellent) but given how long it has been

paid and how UK govt choices spared NI of the 20% unemployment and Troika etc. that Ireland endured it would seem curious as to why UK would keep picking up the tab over a sustained period, why would UK taxpayer agree to that? Surely the 'offset' to losing NI would be a fiscal saving to spend on other UK priorities? It seems asymmetric to say NI could leave, take no cut of the national debt (which has helped NI so much over the decades) and enjoy continued subsidy to keep standard of living high. I think from the UK lens this seems a curious proposition, when it has other parts of the UK crying out for more funding and investment.

APPENDIX FIVE:

LETTER FROM *BRIAN WALKER* AND *OTHERS*

We are civic unionists, more numerous in times of calm, fewer in times of crisis, but more influential than is often realised. We represent the strand of unionism that believes in sustaining civilised life rather than fighting sectarian battles. We embrace human rights and equality and we stand for compromise and reconciliation.

Our identity is Northern Irish, Irish and British in any order of priority. We call all parts of these islands home. Our Britishness is not a false consciousness and we deride the idea of Irishness as foreign. Our passport like our nationality is a matter of choice. The Belfast Agreement is our ideal settlement, not our temporary accommodation. From experience we know this is entirely compatible with moderate nationalism and are convinced it is the right position for unionism to adopt for our own and the common good. But we need help to develop our case from many quarters including Dublin and London.

We believe that dialogue between unionists and nationalists eager to engage can represent positions better than dialogue between committed neutrals, whose conclusions might underestimate the problems. Together at our own initiative and suggested by others, we would develop an agenda both of immediate and long term issues. Our outcomes we hope, will be all the more robust.

A Positive Challenge to Northern Nationalists

"We the undersigned desire a transparent and inclusive debate concerning rights, truth, equality and civil liberties and in so doing challenge assumptions that such values are not embedded within civic unionism, pluralism and other identities.

We are motivated by the desire to build a society for the betterment of everyone. This cannot happen when such a commitment is perceived as being vested in one community or political persuasion. We find it frustrating and puzzling that civic unionism, pluralists and other forms of civic leadership have been rendered invisible in many debates focused on rights and responsibilities. It has reduced our capacity to be heard and undermines the power of reconciliation to shift society away from stale and limiting notions of identity.

We have worked for peace and reconciliation and in so doing have had open and transparent engagement with civic nationalism. That has included recognition of the need for equality and most importantly the urgent need for polarised communities in Northern Ireland to reconcile and deal with barriers to a better future. To achieve this requires the recognition that withholding truth presents as such. This is not unique to any institution or section within our society but where it is a selective process, healing a pernicious and destabilising past remains as a challenge to us all.

Civic unionism, and other identities are not resistant to claims of equality and full citizenship. These identities are central to the development of an authentically fair and tolerant society.

We wish to unite, not divide, and in encouraging transparency we call upon civic nationalism and others to engage with us in frank and fulsome debates about the many values and beliefs that are commonly shared and are vital to transforming the issues that we face".

1. Brian Acheson
2. Ian Acheson
3. Irwin Armstrong
4. Arthur Aughey
5. Stuart Aveyard
6. John Barry
7. Doug Beattie
8. John Bew
9. Elizabeth Boyd
10. Gavin Boyd
11. William Boyd
12. Glenn Bradley
13. Michael Briggs
14. Daniel Brown
15. Jonathan Burgess
16. Paul Burgess

> *A total of 105 people signed the letter, mostly from a unionist background.*

ENDNOTES

QUOTES PAGE

1   https://www.brisbanetimes.com.au/world/europe/more-peaceful-but-facing-uncertainty-northern-ireland-20-years-on-20180409-p4z8i1.html

2   https://www.belfasttelegraph.co.uk/news/northern-ireland/peter-robinson-some-refuse-to-talk-about-the-elephant-in-the-room-but-it-is-positioning-itself-to-squat-upon-their-laps-37179957.html

3   https://www.independent.ie/breaking-news/irish-news/simon-coveney-would-like-to-see-a-united-ireland-in-his-political-lifetime-36347866.html

CHAPTER TWO

4   https://www.health-ni.gov.uk/publications/systems-not-structures-changing-health-and-social-care-full-report

CHAPTER 5

5   https://www.joe.ie/news/i-foresee-a-united-ireland-at-some-point-in-the-future-says-leo-varadkar-557422

6   https://www.independent.ie/breaking-news/irish-news/simon-coveney-would-like-to-see-a-united-ireland-in-his-political-lifetime-36347866.html

7   https://www.politico.eu/article/united-ireland-after-brexit-reunification-vote/

8   https://www.belfasttelegraph.co.uk/news/northern-ireland/peter-robinson-some-refuse-to-talk-about-the-elephant-in-the-room-but-it-is-positioning-itself-to-squat-upon-their-laps-37179957.html

9   'A United Ireland', by Kevin Meagher, published by Biteback
        Publishing, p.297

10   http://cain.ulst.ac.uk/events/peace/docs/dsd151293.htm

11   https://www.belfasttelegraph.co.uk/news/northern-ireland/theresa-
        mays-keynote-address-at-belfasts-waterfront-hall-full-speech-
        37138123.html

12   https://www.belfasttelegraph.co.uk/news/northern-ireland/some-
        unionists-would-prefer-united-ireland-to-brexit-says-powell-
        36786960.html

13   Interview by the author, see above

CHAPTER SIX

14   https://www.independent.co.uk/news/people/ian-paisleys-most-
        caustic-quotes-catholics-breed-like-rabbits-and-multiply-like-vermin-
        9729672.html

15   https://www.telegraph.co.uk/news/2018/08/24/catholic-church-
        dominant-society-says-irish-prime-minister/

16   https://www.cso.ie/en/releasesandpublications/er/pme/
        populationandmigrationestimatesapril2016/

17   https://www.irishcentral.com/roots/history/ireland-ended-its-ban-on-
        divorce-19-years-ago-today

18   https://www.irishcentral.com/roots/history/ireland-ended-its-ban-on-
        divorce-19-years-ago-today

19   https://www.irishtimes.com/life-and-style/ireland-s-divorce-regime-l
        ong-cumbersome-and-expensive-1.2071474

20   https://www.taoiseach.gov.ie/eng/Work_Of_The_Department/
      Programme_for_Government/Programme_for_Government_
      Annual_Report_20181.pdf

21   https://www.theguardian.com/world/2015/may/23/gay-marriage-
      ireland-yes-vote

22   https://www.theguardian.com/world/2015/may/23/gay-marriage-
      ireland-yes-vote

23   The State of Housing in the EU, published by Housing Europe

24   https://www.catholicireland.net/taoiseach-opens-first-new-catholic-
      secondary-school-30-years/

25   https://www.thetablet.co.uk/news/9104/irish-ban-on-priority-places-
      at-catholic-primary-schools

26   https://www.irishtimes.com/business/economy/income-inequality-in-
      ireland-relatively-unchanged-since-crash-1.2880569

27   https://www.maynoothuniversity.ie/sites/default/files/assets/
      document/O%27Connor%20NatTASCreport_0.pdf

28   https://www.gov.uk/income-tax-rates

29   https://www.irishtimes.com/business/personal-finance/ireland-v-the-
      rest-of-the-world-do-we-pay-too-much-tax-1.3230432

30   https://www.professionaladviser.com/professional-
      adviser/news/3026443/uk-state-pension-least-generous-in-the-
      developed-world

31   https://www.socialjustice.ie/content/policy-issues/refundable-tax-
      credits-are-key-dealing-issue-low-pay

CHAPTER SEVEN

32   https://www.health-ni.gov.uk/publications/systems-not-structures-changing-health-and-social-care-full-report

33   http://www.thejournal.ie/national-childrens-hospital-all-island-776109-Jan2013/

34   http://www.catholicherald.co.uk/issues/catholic-herald-app-2018-06-22/will-irelands-catholic-hospitals-defy-varadkar/

35   https://www.irishexaminer.com/ireland/the-illusion-of-power-151017.html

36   https://www.nerinstitute.net/download/pdf/qeo_first_edition_2018_finalcomp.pdf

37   https://webarchive.oireachtas.ie/parliament/media/committees/futureofhealthcare/oireachtas-committee-on-the-future-of-healthcare-slaintecare-report-300517.pdf

38   P156

39   https://ec.europa.eu/health/sites/health/files/state/docs/chp_ir_english.pdf

40   P120

41   P166

42   P127

43   P168

44   P175

45   https://www.nerinstitute.net/download/pdf/qeo_first_edition_2018 _finalcomp.pdf

46   P95

47   P74

48   P73

49   P75

50   Pp115, 116

51   P158

52   Pp80, 81, 99

53   P83

54   P86

55   P154

56   P145

57   P184

58   P102

59   P139

60   https://www.irishtimes.com/news/politics/sl%C3%A1intecare-is-light- at-end-of-the-tunnel-for-health-system-harris-says-1.3590114

61   https://www.fiannafail.ie/ff-response-to-publication-of-slaintecare- implementation-strategy/

62   https://www.irishtimes.com/business/budget/budget-2019-the-full-text-of-paschal-donohoe-s-speech-1.3657270

63   https://www.healthni.gov.uk/sites/default/files/publications/health/expert-panel-full-report.pdf p9

64   https://www.health-ni.gov.uk/sites/default/files/publications/health/expert-panel-full-report.pdf p74/75

CHAPTER EIGHT

65   https://www.irishtimes.com/opinion/northern-ireland-and-the-tripadvisor-index-of-economic-vibrancy-1.3311077

66   https://www.belfasttelegraph.co.uk/opinion/news-analysis/demographics-are-shifting-towards-a-united-ireland-we-must-have-a-plan-35865222.html

67   https://aib.ie/content/dam/aib/investorrelations/docs/economic-research/irish-economy/irish-economic-updates/irish-economy-update-august-2016.pdf

68   https://www.belfasttelegraph.co.uk/business/northern-ireland/economy-watch-just-how-different-are-the-two-economies-on-the-island-of-ireland-37233173.html

69   https://www.quora.com/What-is-the-difference-between-GDP-and-GVA-and-why-GVA-is-more-relevant

70   http://www.cso.ie/px/pxeirestat/Statire/SelectVarVal/saveselections.asp

71   https://www.ons.gov.uk/economy/grossvalueaddedgva/bulletins/regionalgrossvalueaddedincomeapproach/december2015#regional-nuts1-gva-estimates

72   https://www.nisra.gov.uk/statistics/economic-output-statistics/
      gross-value-added

73   http://www.cso.ie/en/releasesandpublications/er/elca/
      earningsandlabourcostsannualdata2016/

74   www.nisra.gov.uk/sites/nisra.gov.uk/files/publications/4xu-NI-ASHE-
      Bulletin-2017.PDF

75   https://www.nisra.gov.uk/statistics/labour-market-and-social-
      welfare/annual-survey-hours-and-earnings

76   also uses median see, https://www.cso.ie/en/releasesandpublications/
      ep/p-syi/psyi2017/econ/earn/

77   http://www.cso.ie/en/releasesandpublications/er/elcq/
      earningsandlabourcostsq32017finalq42017preliminaryestimates/

78   https://www.nisra.gov.uk/statistics/labour-market-and-social-
      welfare/labour-force-survey

79   https://www.cso.ie/en/csolatestnews/pressreleases/2018pressreleases/
      pressstatementlabourforcesurveyq22018/

80   https://www.nisra.gov.uk/news/labour-market-report-july-2018

81   https://www.cso.ie/en/releasesandpublications/er/lfs/
      labourforcesurveyquarter22018/

82   https://www.ucc.ie/en/media/academic/economics/documents/
      research/wp00-3.pdf

83   http://www.assemblyresearchmatters.org/2017/06/14/goods-northern-
      ireland-export-much-worth-go/

84   https://www.economics.ox.ac.uk/materials/working_papers/2828/150-final.pdf

85   ibid

86   https://www.ey.com/ie/en/issues/business-environment/ey-economic-eye-summer-2018

87   http://www.ey.com/ie/en/issues/business-environment/financial-markets-and-economy/economic-eye

88   https://www.centralbank.ie/docs/default-source/publications/quarterly-bulletins/qb-archive/2018/quarterly-bulletin—-q3-2018.pdf?sfvrsn=10

89   https://www.cso.ie/en/releasesandpublications/er/elcq/earningsandlabourcostsq12018finalq22018preliminaryestimates/

90   https://www.cso.ie/en/releasesandpublications/er/lfs/labourforcesurveyquarter22018/

91   https://www.irishtimes.com/business/economy/booming-economy-attracting-new-influx-of-foreign-nationals1.3610131?mode=sample&authfailed=1&pworigin=https%3A%2F%2Fwww.irishtimes.com%2Fbusiness%2Feconomy%2Fbooming-economy-attracting-new-influx-of-foreign-nationals-1.3610131

92   https://www.centralbank.ie/docs/default-source/publications/quarterly-bulletins/qb-archive/2018/quarterly-bulletin—-q3-2018.pdf?sfvrsn=10

93   https://www.centralbank.ie/news/article/strong-growth-forecast-but-take-nothing-for-granted-12-April-2018

94   https://www.theguardian.com/uk-news/2018/jul/19/northern-ireland-close-recession-cbi-warns-may-visits-region

95   https://www.qub.ac.uk/research-centres/
CentreforInternationalBordersResearch/Publications/
WorkingPapers/MappingFrontiersworkingpapers/Filetoupload,
175406,en.pdf

96   http://ec.europa.eu/eurostat/tgm/table.do;jsessionid=4pG0W6-
BXFtjhx_6IF_4G5YrzZ1qOnmk5Wt0GhuR6xUa-vPIeHwj!-
1102445943?tab=table&plugin=1&language=en&pcode=tgs00026

97   http://www.irishborderlands.com/index.html

98   https://academic.oup.com/joeg/article-
abstract/13/6/889/924921?redirectedFrom=fulltext

99   http://blogs.lse.ac.uk/politicsandpolicy/britains-spatially-unbalanced-
economy/

100   https://www.britac.ac.uk/pubs/proc/files/98p035.pdf

101   ibid

102   ibid

103   ibid

104   https://www.economy-ni.gov.uk/sites/default/files/publications/deti/
irep-report.pdf

105   http://www.niassembly.gov.uk/globalassets/documents/enterprise-
trade-and-investment/inquiry—-corp-tax/research-papers/20150319-
assembly-research—-ida-ireland.pdf

106   https://www.idaireland.com/newsroom/end-year-results-2017

107   https://secure.investni.com/static/library/invest-ni/documents/annual-
report-investni-2016-17.pdf

108   https://www.irishtimes.com/news/politics/government-looks-to-push-closer-german-ties-ahead-of-brexit-1.3458515?mode=sample&auth-failed=1&pw-origin=https%3A%2F%2Fwww.irishtimes.com%2Fnews%2Fpolitics%2Fgovernment-looks-to-push-closer-german-ties-ahead-of-brexit-1.3458515

109   U4D, https://www.londonderrychamber.co.uk/.../1403886149—U4D—-need-to-increase-graduates

110   U4D, ibid.

111   U4D, ibid.

112   https://www.pwc.co.uk/who-we-are/regional-sites/northern-ireland/press-releases/northern-ireland-productivity-amongst-lowest-in-the-developed-world.html

113   https://www.ulster.ac.uk/__data/assets/pdf_file/0008/118385/Understanding_productivity_in_Northern_Ireland_27_September_2016.pdf

114   https://www.nerinstitute.net/download/pdf/industrial_policy_wp_2016_061216.pdf

115   https://www.ons.gov.uk/economy/economicoutputandproductivity/productivitymeasures/bulletins/internationalcomparisonsofproductivityfinalestimates/2016

116   https://www.ons.gov.uk/employmentandlabourmarket/peopleinwork/labourproductivity/articles/regionalandsubregionalproductivityintheuk/february2018

117   https://www.ons.gov.uk/employmentandlabourmarket/peopleinwork/labourproductivity/articles/regionalandsubregionalproductivityintheuk/jan2017#results-for-england-scotland-wales-and-northern-ireland-by-nuts3-subregions

118   The ONS Productivity Handbook

119   Northern Ireland competiveness damaged by graduate skills shortage, U4D

120   https://www.nerinstitute.net/download/pdf/industrial_policy_wp _2016_061216.pdf

121   http://eprints.lincoln.ac.uk/7652/1/u4dreportlow-res.pdf

122   https://www.enterpriseresearch.ac.uk/wp-content/uploads/2016/05/GEM-UK-2015-final-report.pdf

123   https://www.fsb.org.uk/docs/default-source/Publications/the-contribution-of-small-businesses-to-northern-ireland.pdf?sfvrsn=1

124   https://www.fsb.org.uk/docs/default-source/Publications/the-contribution-of-small-businesses-to-northern-ireland.pdf?sfvrsn=1

125   https://www.irishtimes.com/business/economy/john-fitzgerald-north-remains-land-of-lost-opportunities-1.3270295

126   https://www.parliament.uk/business/committees/committees-a-z/commons-select/northern-ireland-affairs-committee/news-parliament-2015/electricity-sector-report-published-16-17/

127   http://www.ibec.ie/IBEC/Press/PressPublicationsdoclib3.nsf/vPages/ Newsroom~ibec-cbi-set-out-ambitious-plan-for-all-island-economy-24-07-2016?OpenDocument?OpenDocument

128   http://isni.gov.uk/PDFs/Investment%20Strategy.pdf

129   https://www.per.gov.ie/en/national-development-plan-2018-2027/

130   https://fullfact.org/europe/irish-border-trade/

131   http://www.assemblyresearchmatters.org/2017/06/14/goods-northern-ireland-export-much-worth-go/

132   http://www.bbc.co.uk/news/uk-politics-42223732

133   https://fullfact.org/europe/irish-border-trade/

134   http://www.assemblyresearchmatters.org/2017/06/14/goods-northern-ireland-export-much-worth-go/

135   Department for the Economy briefing on Brexit

136   Department for the Economy briefing on Brexit

137   http://www.assemblyresearchmatters.org/2017/06/14/goods-northern-ireland-export-much-worth-go

138   http://www.assemblyresearchmatters.org/2017/06/14/goods-northern-ireland-export-much-worth-go

139   https://www.irishtimes.com/opinion/a-united-ireland-would-be-worse-off-than-the-republic-1.3010177

CHAPTER NINE

140   https://assets.publishing.service.gov.uk/government/uploads/system/uploads/attachment_data/file/735881/180823_CX_to_Chair_of_TSC_Nicky_Morgan_.pdf

141   https://news.sky.com/story/hit-to-northern-ireland-and-north-east-england-gdp-revealed-in-new-brexit-impact-papers-leak-11240254

142   https://assets.publishing.service.gov.uk/government/uploads/system/uploads/attachment_data/file/735881/180823_CX_to_Chair_of_TSC_Nicky_Morgan_.pdf

143   http://www.europarl.europa.eu/RegData/etudes/BRIE/2017/583116/
       IPOL_BRI(2017)583116_EN.pdf

144   https://www.ufuni.org/farming

145   http://www.europarl.europa.eu/unitedkingdom/en/ukevents/
       brexitstudies.html
       The report cites Aidan Stennett (2016) 'The EU referendum and
       potential implications for Northern Ireland', Northern Ireland
       Assembly Research and Information Service Research Paper, NIAR 32-
       16, p.8.

146   https://www.ons.gov.uk/economy/grossvalueaddedgva/bulletins/
       regionalgrossvalueaddedbalanceduk/1998to2016#wales-was-the-
       fastest-growing-country-in-the-uk-in-2016

147   https://www.nisra.gov.uk/sites/nisra.gov.uk/files/publications/RY6v9-
       labour-market-report-january-2018.PDF

148   Press release from CBI NI

149   https://www.ufuni.org/farming

150   ibid

151   ibid

152   https://www.ft.com/content/cd9323b8-ad0e-11e7-beba-5521c713abf4

153   http://www.irishnews.com/paywall/tsb/irishnews/irishnews/
       irishnews//business/2018/01/16/news/ni-agriculture-subsidies-to-fall-
       after-brexit-warns-report-1232572/content.html

154   https://www.finance-ni.gov.uk/articles/european-structural-and-
       investment-fund-programmes-northern-ireland

155   http://www.niassembly.gov.uk/globalassets/documents/raise/
       publications/2016-2021/2016/aera/6616.pdf

156   ibid

157   https://www.agriland.ie/farming-news/close-to-100-of-uk-farms-
       could-be-worse-off-after-brexit/

158   https://www.economistsforfreetrade.com/wp-
       content/uploads/2017/09/Economists-for-Free-Trade-NME-Paper.pdf

159   https://assets.publishing.service.gov.uk/government/uploads/system/
       uploads/attachment_data/file/684003/future-farming-environment-
       consult-document.pdf

160   http://www.thedetail.tv/articles/the-eu-s-common-agricultural-policy-
       should-we-stay-or-should-we-go

CHAPTER TEN

161   file:///C:/Users/Paul/Downloads/for-everyone.pdf

162   https://www.belfasttelegraph.co.uk/news/northern-ireland/northern-
       ireland-health-service-waiting-times-worst-in-uk-36238914.html

163   http://www.patientclientcouncil.hscni.net/news/view/immediate-and-
       sustainable-solutions-must-be-found-for-hospital-waiting-lists

164   Matt Whittaker, deputy director of Resolution Foundation, tweets
       dated 29 August, 2018

165   https://www.irishtimes.com/business/economy/sustaining-northern-
       standard-of-living-is-a-costly-exercise-1.2597861

166 https://www.belfasttelegraph.co.uk/business/northern-ireland/weve-yet-to-see-the-full-economic-potential-of-the-1998-agreement-36789890.html

167 https://www.thedetail.tv/articles/analysis-brexit-has-split-the-uk-cabinet-but-is-it-also-dividing-communities

168 http://inequalitybriefing.org/graphics/briefing_43_UK_regions_poorest_North_Europe.pdf

CHAPTER ELEVEN

169 http://prcg.com/modeling-irish-unification/report.pdf

170 http://www.euronews.com/2018/02/05/how-fall-of-the-berlin-wall-paved-way-for-germany-s-populists

171 https://www.irishtimes.com/business/economy/john-fitzgerald-north-remains-land-of-lost-opportunities-1.3270295

CHAPTER TWELVE

172 https://www.nerinstitute.net/blog/2015/11/06/the-fiscal-implications-of-irish-unity/ Republished with the permission of Tom Healy

173 http://www.cso.ie/px/pxeirestat/Statire/SelectVarVal/Define.asp?maintable=EHQ10&PLanguage=0

174 https://www.nisra.gov.uk/sites/nisra.gov.uk/files/publications/hY5t1a_20174_Publication%20Document.pdf

175 https://www.nisra.gov.uk/statistics/labour-market-and-social-welfare/annual-survey-hours-and-earnings

176   https://senatormarkdaly.files.wordpress.com/2018/07/research-on-northern-ireland-income-and-expenditure.pdf

177   https://www.cso.ie/en/releasesandpublications/er/giea/governmentincomeandexpenditurejuly2018/

178   https://www.ippr.org/files/2018-03/1521809277_leaving-the-eu-briefing-part2.pdf

CHAPTER FIFTEEN

179   https://www.irishtimes.com/business/economy/united-ireland-would-see-living-standards-in-republic-fall-by-15-1.3629748